A Reflection of Strength

Arnaud Bellevue

iUniverse, Inc.
New York   Bloomington

Copyright © 2010 by Arnaud Bellevue

All rights reserved. No part of this book may be used or reproduced by any means, graphic, electronic, or mechanical, including photocopying, recording, taping or by any information storage retrieval system without the written permission of the publisher except in the case of brief quotations embodied in critical articles and reviews.

iUniverse books may be ordered through booksellers or by contacting:

iUniverse
1663 Liberty Drive
Bloomington, IN 47403
www.iuniverse.com
1-800-Authors (1-800-288-4677)

Because of the dynamic nature of the Internet, any Web addresses or links contained in this book may have changed since publication and may no longer be valid. The views expressed in this work are solely those of the author and do not necessarily reflect the views of the publisher, and the publisher hereby disclaims any responsibility for them.

ISBN: 978-1-4502-1182-6 (sc)
ISBN: 978-1-4502-1183-3 (ebook)
ISBN: 978-1-4502-1184-0 (dj)

Printed in the United States of America

iUniverse rev. date: 03/09/2010

Acknowledgments

I must thank my wife, Tara, for her support during my writing of this memoir. All that I'm able to accomplish in this book is because of her.

I also have to thank my children: Salaam, Latrice, Cherisse, Arnaud Jr., and Jordan. What can I say? Every one of them is a blessing to me, and my life would not be the same without them.

April Davis, my editor, deserves my humble thanks for her understanding, patience, and ability to turn a raw manuscript into a book that I hope you'll enjoy reading. I don't know where I would be if it were not for April. I'm thankful for all she has done.

Hernst, who has inspired me my whole life without uttering a word, is an exemplary older brother. I thank him for his kindness and generosity. I also thank Yanick (Hernst's wife) and their two sons Hernst Jr. and Vladimir.

To my sisters and their husbands: You have been my inspiration, and may God bless. And to my nieces and nephews: I thank you and wish you all well.

I am beyond words for my late mother and father, who laid the foundation that kept me grounded, passed their traditions on to my own children, and raised me in difficult times. Not a day passes in which I don't quietly smile and thank them for all they have done.

To my Aunt Rosemary Carroway, her husband Stacey, and their children: Thank you for always having an open door.

To my co-workers: You have been extraordinarily supportive. On many occasions, I felt as though, had it not been for your support, I wouldn't have overcome the many obstacles I faced. I would especially like to thank Mrs. Vasante Arte, with whom I worked many an afternoon shift, as well as my good friend Paula Guerra for all of her support.

To my best man, William Ortiz, thank you for friendship and all of the valuable time we spent together at the golf course.

To Tyrone Godfrey, author of *1st Thoughts*, thank you for your inspiration.

And a final thanks to all of my friends and coworkers at the Long Island Jewish Medical Center and the LIJ Franklin Hospital, as well as to all others with whom I have worked and who have made a positive impact in my life. Among many others, this list of people includes Dr. Vellozzi, Dr. E. Gugliano, F. Cintron, M. Evellard, M. Mehta, M. Osofsky, L. Desai, M. Fullam, J. Arnold, M. Petelis, S. Jacob, L. Kondabolu, M. Philippe, A. Zarphanelian, C. Tucci, D. Joyas, Basanda Kimiyagaro, and Mohammad Asghar Mirza.

And finally, I would like to use this acknowledgments section to apologize to anyone whom I caused unnecessary pain during my time of confusion and mischief; I pray you accept my deepest apologies, as I truly did not know any better.

Preface

On January 23, 2007, I commenced writing my memoir. I put pen to paper and formally drafted a plan to tell my life's story. This was a challenging task, because I was neither a writer nor a celebrity; however, I had a tale to tell.

Before that point, I had delayed its writing for lack of free time. I became motivated on this date to *make* time, however, after attending the life celebration of a notable person: a man with enormous success, who loved God, and was so many things to so many people. This man was active in his community as a funeral director, a pastor, and a bishop of his church. He was a father, a grandfather, and a goliath to those of us who lived around him.

I, in particular, respected and admired his kindness and gentleness among the general public; whether rich or poor, famous or nameless, young or old, he gave all the respect they deserved.

On this day, sitting in St. Luke's Cathedral in Laurelton Queens, I watched the lifeless body of Bishop Roy L. Gilmore. This was not the first funeral I had attended here, but it had perhaps been the first in which I was sure the deceased had gone to see his master.

As my wife Tara, my daughter Latrice, and I sat waiting for Brother Gilmore's family, clergy, and guest speakers to enter, I was flabbergasted by the rich marble walls and the ornate chandeliers that lined the ceiling, all the way from the pulpit to the last pew of the church. I was equally fascinated by the number of distinguished guests in attendance. St. Luke's Cathedral, it seemed, had become a kingdom of treasures.

Finally the nephew of Reverend Roy Gilmore, the master of ceremonies and one of the pastors at St. Luke's introduced guest speaker Reverend Dr. Floyd H. Flake. Flake was greeted with overwhelming applause as he took the lectern.

Flake had amazing success in our community. As pastor of the Allen African Methodist Episcopal (AME) Church, he also had served the House of Representatives from 1986 to 1997. Prior to his being elected, it seemed we were paying property taxes without representation; our neighborhoods were being financially neglected, as money flowed primarily into other districts. In his term, Reverend Flake helped revitalize Jamaica Queens and began the process of returning it to its former glory as a vibrant community. His work even influenced many who resided in Queens to begin raising families. I was in awe listening to this man of such great stature speaking about the deceased, whom I equally admired.

Flake gazed at the coffin before him, recounting how generous and humble Brother Gilmore had been. The audience clapped often. There was no room for sadness here. This night was a celebration of a life we all admired.

As Reverend Flake concluded, I peered around and noticed friends I had not seen for many years. Some walked a little slower now; several had more gray hair; others were showing the brittleness of old age. Latrice, who sat to my left, must have noticed my observation. She moved closer and asked whether I remembered when the church looked much different. I nodded. Before she had even asked, I had remembered it. Sitting here, watching Reverend Flake, honoring Brother Gilmore, being back in the familiar church, and seeing old faces, I had reflected on many things. In particular, I had begun to wonder how people would remember me when they came to my celebration of life.

Chapter 1

I was born in Croix des Bouquets on September 29, 1954, where my family lived until I was seven or eight. Croix des Bouquets was a northern suburb in the Port au Prince metropolitan area. Port au Prince, the capital of Haiti, was world famous for its exuberant art, which was richly influenced by nature, history, and religion, both Christian and voodoo. The village of Croix des Bouquets exemplified Haitian creativity, resonating with sounds of clanging mallets and sawing chisels in the transformation of raw metal into stunning, often haunting, iron sculpture.

The third child of six to Roland and Yvette Bellevue, my only scant memory of life in Croix des Bouquets is of a big, close-knit family. When I say *big,* I mean inclusive of extended relatives: both sets of grandparents, aunts and uncles and cousins, and my great-grandmother.

My grandmother and great-grandmother from my mom's side were both farmers. They grew crops, raised poultry, and sold their products at the local outdoor market. Grandmother Lucene's property consisted of a big house, some smaller hut houses, and another medium-size house where my aunt and cousins lived. The backyard farm was filled with sugar cane, mangoes, bananas, coconuts, and other vegetables.

Even as young as I was, I remember going behind Lucene as she collected her crops with a straw-woven basket, often pulling me out of her way with her free arm whenever I would interrupt. I had fun as we walked together through the fields back to her house. At the farm, I rode the big pigs, chased the goats, and watched the animals at slaughter. There was also a big area in the yard where I chased whatever chicken she was about to make into meat to sell at the market.

Although it was a long way to the market, I was allowed to take the trip with my great-grandmother, Victoire, who, more skillfully than my grandmother carried her straw basket atop her head, leaving both hands free.

Behind Lucene's house there was a little dirt alley lined with coconut trees, which led to the river that irrigated the crops. On occasions, in the early morning, I would go with Lucene to collect water. She would treat the water with aloe and put the water in a big jug, and that would be water for cooking and drinking. She would always stop to fix something as we walked along the dirt path that led us to Grand Rigol, the local name for the manmade river that ran from the mountains and passed Lucene's farm. When the tides were high, Hernst, three of my cousins, and I would go for mid-afternoon swims; when the tides were low, we could practically catch fish, shrimp, and small crabs with our hands.

My paternal grandfather made iron sculptures, which he sold for a living at the outdoor market. I would watch him bang on a piece of hot metal, shaping it into a horseshoe-shaped object. I knew he did not want me close to him while he was working, because sparks would fly from the hot iron. But I would wait for him to ask me to move, and then would do so only for candy money.

My parents lived walking distance from my grandparents' houses, so at night, we would all sit in the courtyard outside Lucene's house, enjoying the moon and the stars, and telling jokes. We'd often stay until we fell asleep. Then a little later, we'd awake and go home to bed. During blackouts, which were common during the night, we would listen to the faraway beating of drums and the singing of Haitian gospel music; it was the voodoo ceremony that took place near Lucene's backyard. We kids were not allowed to observe the voodoo ceremonies. Instead, we followed the Catholic faith. My cousins and I had to attend church nearly every Sunday to prepare for our first communion, and Lucene always took us to the early morning services.

I was typically an early riser anyway, though mostly so I could negotiate money out of my dad's clients. When I was around seven, my dad worked for the city as the controller of irrigation. It seemed there was always someone in our living room very early, waiting to discuss business matters with him. It didn't take me long to realize that if I was up early enough to greet the client first, I could often earn a penny or two for letting my dad know the client was waiting. This allowed me to go to the corner store for bubble gum. I would then walk over to my aunt's house to share the bubble gum with my cousins.

On days when there were no clients, while my dad was still sleeping, I would go play with the steering wheel inside his car. One day, while doing this, I pressed the clutch. Before I realized it, the car was moving. It rolled forward down the sloped driveway, toward the basin full of water that was our swimming pool. My brother, Hernst, yelled for me to stop. My father came out just in time to get in front of the car and, with his bare hands, stopped it from falling into the pool.

I was in shock. I hadn't realized what I had done until he pulled me out of the car. When I began crying, he picked me up, put me on his shoulder, and instead of giving me a spanking, he gently patted my back. From then on, my dad locked his car doors. He also moved the basin away from the driveway.

◆ ◆ ◆

When I was eight years old, my parents decided they wanted us kids to go to better schools. So when my dad lost his job with the city, they took the opportunity to move us to Port au Prince, which was about ten miles away. My dad got a new job, and my mom, who had always been a homemaker, opened a small convenience store in the front room of our house.

Living in the city was a major change for me because I was accustomed to rural life.

In Port au Prince, Hernst and I attended a private, all-boy Catholic school called Heart of Jesus. We spoke French at school, even though, in the streets and at home, we spoke Creole. Further, we were required to perform the ritual of all Catholics around the world—Mass—in Latin.

I received my first Communion at Heart of Jesus, after giving the history of the saint I had studied and then explaining the life of the Catholic church. I had always looked forward to my first Communion; I'd thought it was a sign that I was a good Catholic.

Every Saturday afternoon, I would go to observe Afternoon Mass and confess to a priest all the evil I had done that week. Then every Sunday, our class would walk in double-file from the school in Rue Montalais to the huge cathedral where we would attend Mass and I would receive the Sacrament of Baptism during Communion.

Sunday Mass was usually followed with the best meal of the week. Mom would prepare my favorite dish: chicken and red snapper, cooked Haitian style, with white rice and red or black bean sauce.

◆ ◆ ◆

I was the rascal of my family. I was always in trouble either for playing soccer (called football) in the street or for not knowing my lesson.

One morning, breakfast was taking a little longer than usual, and becoming impatient, I kicked the portable stove filled with hot coal. One of the coals dropped inside my right boot. I screamed, but no one knew why. They thought I was just being mischievous as usual. Finally, my mom noticed the smoke coming from my right boot and poured water into it, but not before the coal had left its permanent mark on my foot.

Another time, I returned from school to find all of my clothes gone. My father had taken them and given me only my older sister's dress to wear. This was an attempt to get me to stay inside after school and study instead of playing soccer in the streets. Dad did not like the idea of my playing soccer before I studied my lessons because he wanted me to become a doctor, lawyer, or engineer, the professions that most working middle-class Haitians wanted for their children. Not wanting me to follow the footsteps of a great soccer star, my dad only allowed me to play on the porch or in the backyard. I would get in trouble every time I was caught playing in a scrimmage with the neighborhood kids.

Giving me only a dress to wear after school worked for a few days, just until I'd had time to gather enough coins to bribe the maid. I convinced her to hide a pair of shorts for me behind the refrigerator. The following afternoon, after school, instead of going to my room to study my lesson, I went behind the refrigerator, exchanged my sister's dress for the shorts, and went out to play soccer with the kids.

As usual, our game drew the neighborhood crowd, who stood around, watching and cheering us on. At the end of the game, I scored the winning goal, and the group held me up to celebrate. When they did, I looked up, and locked eyes with my father, who was just walking home from work. When I got to the house, he gave me a whipping.

Another time I got punished for being out in the streets, it had nothing to do with soccer. You see, our house was just a few blocks from the presidential palace. We were so close to the palace, in fact, that we had to salute the Haitian flag when it went up in the morning, as well as in the evening when it came down. From our front door, we could see the guards patrolling the palace.

As a result, all of the attractions that made their way to the palace passed in front of our house. The big annual attraction, of course, was Mardi Gras. Bands on a moving truck played wild music and fans followed, dancing in the street, wearing crazy costumes, and engaging in mischievous behavior. Well, one Sunday morning, such a band passed in front of our house, and

I followed the music. It didn't take long for Hernst, who was responsible for me but could not tell our father where I was at the moment, to be punished, after which he came into the crowd to find me. With my shirt raised over my head and my hips rotating to the cadence of the music, I didn't see him coming. Before I knew it, Hernst had sucker-punched me and pulled me out of the crowd. I was ready to throw some punches until he said Father was home looking for me. I must have gotten a beating, but it was all worth the fun.

◆ ◆ ◆

There was never a day in my life where we did not have what we wanted to eat. And Dad was able to afford a maid and a butler. But that was not enough for his family. As he looked toward the future, he saw no advancement for his children, so he began making plans to enter the United States. Meanwhile, he sent us to Grandmother's for summer vacation, which kept with the family tradition and gave my mom a break. Besides, he did not want us in the big city when we were out of school.

I loved summer vacation. There were no lessons to recite, and I was free from all the chaos and limitations of city life. At Grandma's, life moved at a slower pace. We had a dirt yard, lots of trees, and fresh air, and we played all day long. Hernst and I loved to travel to the rural area, which had my favorite mangoes, coconuts, bananas, and other fruits and vegetables.

One summer vacation, I began to experience the maturity of my manhood, though without my knowledge. Every time I woke up and then at other times throughout the day, my penis would get so hard it hurt, but I did not know why. Sometimes it hurt so much, I would bang it against a banana tree to get it to stop, but it would not.

One time, while Hernst, my cousin, and I were swimming at the lake, it got hard. Not wanting anybody to notice, I ran to a coconut tree. After a few minutes of banging at the coconut tree, Hernst and my cousin found me. I had a horrible reputation for the rest of that summer: "Arnaud, horny bastard," they'd say. "He was humping the coconut tree!"

I was so embarrassed about the incident that I ran to Lucene. I knew she loved me, and I felt that she would never misguide me. As usual, she was calm; just being around her gave me sanctuary and the assurance that no one would bother me.

That was my last summer vacation at Grandmother Lucene's. After that, in 1965, President Francois Duvalier proclaimed himself president for life. That was when my dad became positive that there would be no more opportunity for us in Haiti, and so he made his quiet exit. He got a permanent visa and left for America to fulfill the requirement for obtaining permanent resident status: finding a job and proving to the American embassy that he could provide food and shelter for his family, who was to follow.

Then one morning, Mom got us all dressed up and took us to the American embassy. There, she filled out forms and answered questions from a man who also directed a few simple queries to us kids.

A few months after that, we got dressed and went to the airport. And that was the last time I saw my country.

Chapter 2

The Immigration Act of 1965 made it easier for my father to send for us. Designed as a result of the civil rights movement, aimed at ridding America of racial discrimination, the act increased the quota of people who could enter the United States from third-world countries. Immigrants were granted residency based on skills and education. After the Immigration Act was signed by President Lyndon Johnson, immigrants who had previously been denied entry to the United States were able to move there.

My mother, my sisters, Hernst, and I spent a night in Florida, waiting for our transfer flight to JFK airport. When we landed at JFK the next day, December 5, 1965, my father was waiting for us. We had not seen him in nine months.

We arrived in Brownsville Brooklyn around lunchtime, at our one-bedroom apartment. And thus my life in America began at the age of eleven.

Things were very different here. We were in an unfamiliar place. We did not know anyone or speak the language. The winter months were harsh, too, as we were not used to cold weather. Suddenly, we could not wear the short-sleeve shirts and short dress pants that we were accustomed to.

Back home, I'd had a sense of ownership. Every morning, I'd wake up to breakfast on the table and freshly ironed school clothes. All I had to do was wash up and head to school. At lunch, I walked home from school, which was on the same block, to a prepared dining room table. There, we were taught proper table etiquette, morality, and respect. We ate our protein and our vegetables and our carbohydrates.

Back home, dinner had been different too. We ate light meat, and then recited our lessons to our mom. Mom stayed at home to care for us, and she had various helpers. These helpers were younger women looking for better opportunities. Thus, they would find jobs from families who could afford to pay them and provide them with places to sleep. They usually lived in the countryside, and would come to the city on the weekdays to work, traveling back home on the weekends; some, however, stayed the entire month.

This was the lifestyle my family was accustomed to in Haiti, and it no longer existed when we moved to America. A Haitian singer once wrote that Haiti is a sweet country, which he loved very much, but it had no evolution. My father shared his thoughts. Although, for him, life was as sweet as honey, he felt his children deserved better. Coming to America, he thought, was an opportunity to give us what we deserved.

Too young to understand, I shed many tears in our one-bedroom apartment. Weeping was also very common among Hernst and my sisters. Our parents did their best to help us adjust to America, but all I could see was that in Haiti, I'd had a sense of belonging. All I could see was that my dreams there had been without limitation. And in America, I felt none of that. I did not understand until much later that I had been the exception to the Haitian standard of living. I did not understand that, though there were other kids who were more privileged than I, most of Haiti was poor and desolate.

Having a mother and father who wanted to see their children excel beyond that desolation led us to flee a tropical country to a place where everything we did was contained within walls.

◆ ◆ ◆

Our apartment building was owned by a Jewish gentleman. Every month on Friday afternoon before Shabbat, he would collect his rent and a plate of freshly-cooked Haitian food. My mother never showed that she was worried about our current situation because my parents had plans for us. They had expected the beginning to be rough and knew it would only get better through hard work.

My father and some of his friends worked in jobs other than their professions to maintain their families financially. Usually these jobs had low pay and long hours. My father, once a civil engineer in Haiti, now worked as a truck driver. Others became cab drivers, factory workers, and housekeepers.

It was convenient that all of the tenants who lived in our building came to America because of the common goal of opportunity, and worked in whatever jobs were available to them in order to fulfill that American dream. In this way, all of the tenants at 32a Sutter Avenue became friends. We helped one another because our cultures were similar. We shared food and jokes as we stood in front of the building on hot summer afternoons, listening to the same music and often going to the same parties, where they served Haitian rum and *griot* (fried pork cooked with Haitian spices).

The neighborhood was changing. Immigrants who had been there for years—the Jews, Italians, and others who lived in Brownsville—were moving out to better areas of Brooklyn, or to Staten Island, Queens, and Upstate New York. Having, by then, been in America long enough to make the money needed to enjoy better lives, they moved to places that gave them more than what Sutter Avenue had to offer. They moved to bigger homes, better school districts, and areas where they felt safer.

In turn, the previous immigrants—at least those who did not reject the entry of new people—sold or rented housing to the new immigrants from the West Indies, South America, Africa, and Asia, who came seeking out better opportunities for their families.

◆ ◆ ◆

We were here to work hard, and my task was to go to school and learn a new language—a language very different than to what I was accustomed.

We kids did not register to go to school until months after we had arrived. A Spanish lady in our building took us to register at Public School 189, the elementary school for the district in which we lived. By then, the semester was almost over, so Hernst and I ended up repeating the whole year, though my older sister was able to move up to the next grade.

I sounded different when I tried to read what was written, and I would get looks from my listeners as if I was not as intelligent as they because of my pronunciation. Kids my age called me names, laughed at me, and made jokes about me behind my back. They gave me the nickname Frenchie because of my heavy accent, which they apparently did not know was Haitian. I think most of them just wanted someone to make fun of, and because I sounded different than they, I was it.

In seventh grade, a boy named Little John would follow me every afternoon after school and call me Frenchie. They called him Little John because he was chubby. He was definitely bigger than me, as I had a small frame. Still, I decided one day that I had enough of this bully, and I was ready to do whatever I had to, to stop him—even if that meant getting beat up. I let him carry on his usual harassment until we approached the corner of the block farthest from our school. There, I stopped, turned around, and called him names in return. He did not like it, and we both prepared to fight.

Before Little John threw the first punch, I surprised him with a soccer-style kick that threw his balance. He landed on the ground looking up at me. While everyone watched, I slapped him a few times, then I walked away.

◆ ◆ ◆

My struggles did not end on the school grounds. I could not understand any of the sports I watched on television, and that was if I could even find a game. The first time I flipped through the television guide that Mom had picked up from the grocery store, I had to spell out f-o-o-t-b-a-l-l to myself first in order to identify the word in writing. When I finally found it, I saw that a game was scheduled for Sunday afternoon. I was so excited for Sunday to come, but when it did, I learned that this was not the same football I had grown up playing.

I had some reprieve from unfamiliarity on Saturdays, when we would walk from our apartment down to Belmont Avenue, while Dad worked his sixteen-hour shift. There, we shopped at an outdoor market like the one we'd gone to in Haiti. All of the merchants would be lined up, some with big barrels of fire to provide heat for the day. My mother would always need our help speaking to the corner butcher in sign language, and we would commonly run into someone we knew.

All of the produce there was fresh and unprocessed. We bought live chicken, and I watched as the merchants slaughtered it, plucked it, and cut it as my mother wanted. She always took the head and the neck bone because I liked the neck bone and my older sister liked the head.

And it is worth saying that not all unfamiliarity was negative. I could not believe the first time I saw snow. It was only a flurry, but I was so excited. I ran out of our apartment, down the hallway to the front entrance of the building. I opened the door and stood on the sidewalk without a coat, letting the flurries hit my face, and trying to eat them. I jumped with excitement and stayed as long as I could until I began to get extremely cold. When I tried to open the door to go back in, the door was locked, and I did not have a key. I had to ring the doorbell and disturb my parents.

It was not easy as we mixed in this new culture in America. Back home we had help doing everything. In America, we had to learn how to do things on our own.

Chapter 3

While I was at PS 189 on East New York Avenue in Brooklyn, Hernst and my older sister went to junior high and high school, and my younger siblings stayed at home.

In school, I became classified as an ESL student—or a foreigner for whom English was a Second Language. So in English class, I was joined by many other students from different countries. Being among familiar company made me more comfortable, prompting me to speak more in that class and even ask questions. In my other classes, I did not speak any English, because whenever I said even the simplest word, the entire class would laugh. Little did they know they sounded equally as funny to me. Soon, I became a joker, thinking everything was funny.

The only class I excelled in was math, because numbers were easy for me and I didn't have to piece together even one full English sentence. All I had to do was pick up a piece of chalk, and everyone paid attention. Most of them even copied my answers from the blackboard because I was better at the subject than they were.

With my parents struggling—my dad working endless hours and my mom at home without any help—I no longer had anyone to help me to the extent I was used to. There was no one to help me recite or even do my school work. As a result, I began to really test the limits of this new school culture of mine. I became amazed at how much students could get away with here. In particular, I couldn't believe they would not get a whipping for neglecting their homework. In Haiti, the first time students did not do their homework, the teacher whipped them, and the second time, the principal whipped them. I discovered that students in America had rights, and teachers were not allowed to touch them.

After being in a system that was so disciplined, I concluded this new school system was easy. All I had to do was sit and keep quiet, and I would get by.

◆ ◆ ◆

I found a good friend in a boy named Gerald. Gerald also spoke Creole, so he and I had similar experiences in school, learning to speak our new language. We would communicate in Creole during school hours, and then began hanging out after school at the nearby park, shooting basketball or throwing the football.

At one point, we also started playing punch ball. Gerald's little brother Philipp had become acclimated to this new game and introduced it to us. We would play on the cement baseball field and use fielders, as if playing baseball. The "puncher" would hit the ball as hard as he could, and if no one caught it or tagged him, he would run home and score. Sometimes, we'd have a full field of players for this game.

It was not long before I also became acclimate to the new sports at school. First, Hernst and I watched a lot of football, basketball, and baseball on television. Second, we were exposed to all of these major sports at Lincoln Terrace Park. This huge park was walking distance to many parts of Brooklyn, including the area where I lived. My friends from the neighborhood would gather there on Sunday, put up two makeshift goals, and start a game of soccer.

When not playing sports, I'd walk through the giant park and look for other things to do. On many occasions, I got lost doing just such a thing. The park attraction that I particularly enjoyed was the swings. I would do tricks on them, and we would have contests to see who could swing the highest and the longest.

◆ ◆ ◆

The summer before I entered junior high school, the neighbor's granddaughter came to stay with her grandmother for the weekend. I first met Laila by the mailbox. She was a pretty girl about my age. She had long hair, light brown eyes, and skin that looked to have not been in the sun much. She gave me a welcoming smile, as if she wanted to be friends, but I could not say much in response.

The next day around the same time, I rushed to get the mailbox key, but someone else in our apartment had already taken it. I rushed to the mailboxes to see if it had been Laila. There she was, taking out her grandmother's mail. She stopped and looked over her shoulder at me. Then with her welcoming smile, she asked me something I could not understand. I replied to her in the way I responded to most English-speaking people—"I don't understand. Please speak slowly"—and she did.

After answering her question the best I could, I told her I spoke French. She tried saying something in French, and I repeated what she said, but with more correct pronunciation. Then I told her, "If you teach me English, I will teach you French." Thus was the beginning of our lessons under the steps.

Since, I learned, that she visited her grandmother every weekend, we managed to meet under the steps at different times throughout the summer. Every weekend, she would be there waiting, and when she saw me approach, she'd put a finger over her lips, as if giving me a secret sign. It did not take long before she became someone I really liked and wanted to be around, and it seemed she enjoyed my company the same.

One day, our friendship reached a new level when I asked her how to say *lips* in English and she asked me how to kiss in French. And with that, I held her in my arms and kissed her. This became a regular occurrence at our meetings, until one day, we decided to go up to the roof to make out. When we got there, though, we decided we were too scared to make out, and immediately ran back down to the ground level.

Another time, she wanted to meet on a Sunday afternoon instead of the usual Saturday. I knew that time was usually very quiet in the area, with no one dropping off or picking up mail. As I approached her, the way I had many other times, she had her finger over her lips. But then she looked right at the bulk I always had in my pants and whispered, "Let me see."

I felt the pain I'd experienced in Haiti, those times when I'd bang a tree so the hardness would go away. She repeated quietly, "Let me see." I moved closer to her and looked around, making sure we were at the far end under the stair well, where no one could possibly see us. I unzipped my shorts and pulled them down to my knees. Laila's eyes lit up, and she slowly closed them and opened them again. I looked at my penis standing up, glued to my stomach, then I raised my head toward Laila. For the first time, I noticed she had dimples when she smiled.

I moved closer to her, and she retreated to the corner on the floor, the look in her eyes welcoming the opportunity for anything to happen. Then she touched me and pulled me closer. I had never been in this kind of situation, but it felt natural.

She was so close to me now that I could feel her breath on me and her heart pumping. My mind was racing, wondering what I should do. I could not bang her like I used to bang the banana tree. I discovered, though, that I did not want to bang her. Instead, I wanted to lay it gently on her. As I did, I started to rub it against her body. That's when we heard a voice.

"What are you doing here? Get away from there!"

We jumped and looked. It was the superintendent of the building. I didn't know how long he had been watching us.

Leila got up and ran straight to her grandmother's apartment. The superintendent must have said something to her grandmother after that, because later, I heard her crying.

◆ ◆ ◆

During my three years at JHS 232, I met a lot of people and learned things that had a major effect on my later life. In fact, my time in junior high school would become the foundation of my life in America.

My first junior high friendship, with a guy named Patrick who was also from Haiti, started on a rocky note, because some girl I walked home ended up liking him instead. Many girls liked Patrick. He was older than I was and considered a ladies' man.

After we moved past the girl incident, we became good friends. We found out we had come to America from Haiti at about the same time. When I eventually told Patrick about my experience with women, the extent of which was that summer with Laila, he looked at me as if I were crazy and said, "That ain't no sex." Then he promised me that one day we would get me "a real woman."

Already, the women he hung out with liked me, too, even though I was a couple of years younger than they were. At an early age, I started going to basement parties and gathering at the local pool hall with older guys to talk about the women we had met.

My immediate love in all of this new socializing became rhythm and blues. I was a master at keeping with the music during a slow dance, intertwining my body with my partner's using all kinds of highly flexible moves. The women I danced with would get excited and ask if I wanted to make out and get down. To me, getting down meant merely not breaking my stride.

But for every point I scored in slow dancing, I lost one with my father, when he discovered I had been sneaking out at night. (I usually would keep a window open, so I could leave through it without making a noise after everyone had gone to bed. One night my father found out, and he closed the window and waited by it, until I got there.)

On top of that, I lost double points—both with my father and in school—for becoming more interested in the opposite sex than in my studies. This was the point at which I found myself between two powerful forces. I had two groups of friends: one chased women and did not want to go to school; the other played soccer and wanted a future. And then there was a third party—my parents, or, actually, my father in particular—who wanted me to do well in school but was against my playing sports altogether. He believed that to contribute to society, you must be a doctor, lawyer, engineer, or any other kind of professional who needs a higher degree.

Different sides won out at different times. There were times I would not go to class or just barely pass. However, I did pass, because the other force that told me I had to achieve would later take over. Those years, I discovered a lot about myself, not the least of which was that if I wanted to follow my childhood dreams of becoming a professional soccer player, I had to go to school.

Fortunately, I had some teachers who made the school experience a bit easier than it could have been. My ninth grade hygiene teacher caught my attention one day when he talked about sexually transmitted diseases; syphilis, in particular. Because of all the smooching I had been doing, I posed many questions. After answering many of them, he asked whether I had been with a woman. Of course I would not admit anything in front of the class. But, after class I stayed and had a discussion with him. To this day, I think that our discussion probably saved my life. He assured me that kissing would not cause me to have syphilis, but then gave me a look that seemed to say, "From where you are now, penetration is the next step." And then he introduced me to a condom. He told me that if I decided to penetrate, I should use it as protection. He was a cool guy and did not judge me. He also spoke with authority and experience, so I listened and stored the information he gave.

My junior high science teacher was also cool. He was a young guy with long hair, and he was good at soccer. So he and I got together after school one day and decided to start a soccer team with the class. It was a great experience for all of us, because most of us were from Haiti and had a lot of experience playing the game.

After winning the entire season, we lost the final game by one goal because of the many rules the parents and coaches had made up that had nothing to do with soccer. The parents of the kids from the other team controlled the game, acting as line judges and referees. That's not to say their players didn't have skills, but they could not have won if the referee had not disqualified two of our goals at the request of parents.

When our team argued with the referee about what we thought were unfair calls, I wished my parents would have been as involved as the parents from the other team. As for my parents, they did not understand that giving that kind of support, for one, and they were too busy working to buy a house so that we could move on to a better life. I had not even told them about this wonderful soccer experience.

That was my first loss, and it showed me that regardless of how good you are, there are always external forces greater than you. However, we did have fun.

During the season, after every game we had played, the principal would announce the final score and name everyone on our team who had scored. My name was mentioned often because I scored in every game. One of my teachers used this to try to help me, because I was not performing well in her class; I missed homework assignments, and barely passed tests. So she told me, "Every point you make in soccer, you lose in my class." She was trying to motivate me, because she knew I had the potential to do better.

◆ ◆ ◆

In 1968, the assassinations of Dr. Martin Luther King Jr. and Robert Kennedy opened my eyes. In fact, I was not even aware of what some Americans thought of the black race until after Dr. King's death.

I remember specifically that my family and I were in our apartment watching our black-and-white television when we heard the news. But as a teenager fresh from another country,

I did not understand what a profound blow the assassination would have on our community. I didn't understand until the next day at school, when everyone was talking about it.

In the weeks that followed, I heard the "I Have a Dream" speech for the very first time, as it was being repeated over and over on the black-and-white TV Dad had just purchased. Although I could not understand what was being said, I knew that nearly everyone around me considered the speech significant, so I consulted the dictionary to learn about words such as *segregation, desegregation, citizenship rights,* and *protest.* It was then that I began to understand exactly who Dr. King was. I learned that he and his associates had organized peaceful demonstrations to show conformity with the Declaration of Independence, and that Dr. King, a Baptist minister, had lost his life because he was a huge force in the push for racial equality.

After that, I began to learn about other civil leaders of the time and to listen to other speakers who emerged, talking about the many ways racism could affect me in America. I really began to understand the difference between being black and being white in this country.

I also, however, began to form my own, somewhat different, opinions on the matter. Unlike many others, I did not think of Dr. King's cause as racial—as one of white against black. I saw it, instead, as an issue of oppression. Haiti was a nation where everyone was black and similarly oppressed. So to me, Dr. King was beyond color; he demonstrated for people who were oppressed regardless of color, sex, or religion.

Further, the message of Dr. King was synonymous with that of my dad, who always told me that to be equal I must put forth my best effort. My dad, like King, exemplified that philosophy as well. He put in long hours, always willing to sacrifice for his family with hard work and discipline. And he made us kids put forth our best, just as he did.

As a response to Dr. King's assassination, rioters went into stores, destroying merchandise and taking things that did not belong to them. People looked at me as if I were crazy when I did not join them in the rioting. This was confusing to me, as Dr. King was an advocate of change through peaceful and orderly demonstrations. I could never take or destroy anything that was not mine. When Dr. King talked about content of character, I felt as if he were talking about me.

All of this unrest, in combination with that surrounding the assassination of Robert Kennedy and our presence in the Vietnam War, was unsettling to me. I did not understand why all of this killing was taking place. During these troubled times, it was difficult to think of the future because it seemed apparent that anyone could lose his life so quickly. In that way, Dr. King's death was the simply the beginning of what was to come.

Chapter 4

In the summer of 1969, just before my fifteenth birthday, I became involved with a soccer team of older players from Haiti. Though I was too young to play for them officially, I watched them to learn all I could about the sport, and they allowed me to play games under the names of any absent players.

In those days, soccer in Haiti was more advanced than that in the United States. In international competitions, Haitian soccer teams beat U.S. teams all the time. So I always wished my parents had been more supportive of my playing soccer. My mom always said that she knew I loved soccer from the time I was in her belly, because while she was pregnant, I would never stop moving. But that was the extent of what my parents said about it. I wished, instead, that they'd see my talent, say America was not where I should be because soccer was not popular here, and move me back to Haiti—or to any other country that appreciated the sport more than this one.

I could not blame my parents for not supporting me in soccer, however; even the Haitian soccer player who I had admired as a child did not meet their standards of being successful. You see, in Haiti, soccer players were poor; most didn't have professions other than soccer, and that did not pay. And when these players got inevitable sports injuries, that would be it. Most of them, without degrees, would be at the bottom of society.

Still, whenever I watched European soccer on TV, I saw excitement among the fans. Brazilian and Argentinean fans seemed equally thrilled by the game. Those people loved soccer as much as I did. And it was always highly publicized how successful these players were and how much money they made. Maybe if I was in another country, I thought, I would get the support I needed to have just a chance of becoming a great player.

By my first year in high school, I was playing with and against international players, though the leagues were not professional; there just happened to be enough ethnic groups in the New York area to form summer leagues after the formal winter league was over.

Seeing an opportunity, some of we older players formed our own Haitian league. The team I was on, called Victory, was one of many representing Brooklyn. Our league rented high school soccer fields for games and even charged spectators. Before long, we were the summer Sunday-afternoon entertainment for the Haitian community. When the New York Cosmos were starting out in the late 1970s, we shared Hofstra University in Uniondale, Long Island, and drew more people than even they could. It was a fantastic experience.

I had gained experience in one position: right back. In soccer, the right back is a defensive position on the right side of the field that allows the player to also participate as an offensive player. The most common formation was the 4-2-4, which meant a team played with four forwards, two midfields, and four defenders. Each defender's job was to stop the other team from scoring, so we would all line up in front of the goalie.

The Haitian press even began using the few back pages of its newspaper to cover the games. Because of the position I played, I usually appeared in a picture somewhere guarding one of the many international players on the opposing team. As a result, I became well-known among those who read the paper and attended the games.

Eventually, some of us joined the under-eighteen league, called the Eastern District League in our area, which we played in the spring and fall. Every Sunday, Lionel Charles, a Haitian guy we called Charlie, would pick us up and take us to Van Courtland Park in the Bronx to practice. It was usually he and his wife,

Mommy, of Spanish descent. Charlie, who spoke fluent Spanish, was a factory worker whose pride and joy was to have us play in the tournament. The teams in that tournament in the early 1970s were primarily South American and European teams.

Mommy and Charlie picked us up twice a week for practice and games, regardless of the weather, and they always gave us their all. When we won, they celebrated. When we lost, they encouraged us to do better next time. When the referee made a call against us, they argued our position. They made us feel like a team, and they kept us grounded. And for me personally, they provided a sense of belonging to a group that wanted to do positive things. When I was looking for refuge from my playboy days, they would give me sanctuary. And they gave me an opportunity to work on my game, sharing a sport with me that even my parents did not share. I never understood what they got out of all the effort they put forth; I could only hope the journey was as rewarding to them as it was to me.

The opportunity to play soccer in my teens was a blessing. It gave me a sense of belonging and of working hard at something. And my teammates and other friends who played soccer, who were all students, were also the part of my life that kept me in school. They had the ability to pull me back and make me aware that there were other enjoyments in life besides being with the ladies. Although they were also there to applaud me on all of the nice and beautiful women who came to our games.

◆ ◆ ◆

More and more, my name was announced over the school loudspeaker at George Wingate High School. This made me proud, not to mention popular with the girls—not the girls from Patrick's crowd, but those in my class who were my age. These girls would come to the games just to check me out.

Unfortunately, with my increasing popularity, I began skipping out on classes. In fact, I very rarely went to school except on test days. As a result, I failed too many classes and became academically ineligible to play soccer my senior year.

My parents decided to transfer me to South Shore High School. In a way, the soccer coach recruited me; South Shore was placed in the first division, and the coach was looking for good players. After my transfer, he held a meeting with the team and told them I would not be able to play with them that year because of academic reasons. But he also announced that he wanted to provide help for me, so that I could do better and join the team as a "super senior."

I felt very uncomfortable, because the majority of the kids did not want me there, and, at that time, the feeling was mutual. Whereas George Wingate High School was becoming predominately black, as many students from the Islands, Jamaica, Haiti, and Trinidad moved into that district, South Shore was in a white neighborhood. The student population was predominately made up of Italian and Jewish immigrants who had entered the States much earlier than the Caribbean students at Wingate.

These students opposed "outsiders" who were allowed to come to their school. They held several demonstrations, usually covered by the media, in which they held baseball bats and told TV reporters that "these kids need to go back to their own district." On several occasions, these people were parents, who would chase the "other" kids off with their bats.

Seeing how advanced South Shore was compared to Wingate was my first glance at the unequal distribution of wealth in Brooklyn. I could not believe how large the hallways, classes, and gym were in my new school, and the soccer field was in perfect condition; it even had Astroturf. Then, when I started going to class, I really saw what those parents on TV had been defending. The school environment here was completely different than what I was used to: the books were brand new, and the teachers dressed well and talked respectfully to students. At Wingate, teachers told me things like, "You're going to be a jailbird," or, "You're not going to make it." The teachers at South Shore embraced me and gave me all of the help I needed to achieve my goal of graduating. This completely different experience made me realize why everyone was fighting. The haves wanted to keep what they had; the have-nots wanted to get what they deserved.

After I left Wingate, I really concentrated on doing what I needed in order to graduate. I was not behind in years, but at that point, I did not have enough credits to be a senior in my senior year. To catch up, I registered for more than the usual amount of classes during the day and also took night school. Once, a teacher who knew about my extra workload, while passing me in the hallway, said, "You are Arnaud! You can be whatever you want to be."

This teacher's encouragement was well-intended, and I took it seriously to follow the curriculum. Whatever did not happen at Wingate, I made sure happened at South Shore. I learned from every bad experience I'd had and made up for it. I even took a night-school class, upon the recommendation of my guidance counselor, so that I could join the January graduating class instead of waiting for June. Still, my grades were not great. I would often do only what was necessary to pass. I did not change my playboy attitude either. I was not skipping class to hang out as often, but weekends were still for clubs and parties and chasing girls.

By then, Patrick and I started hanging out with a guy named Yves, who I had met back at Wingate. He, too, was older than I, and always had many women hanging around him. With so many guys away fighting in Vietnam War, it seems lonely women were all over the place. So when the three of us went to parties together, it would be a competition to see who could score first. I was always the last one, because Patrick and Yves did not care who they scored with. If it had legs, the right sex organ, and the willingness, they would be on top doing their thing. I needed to get to know a woman, to get them excited. If I liked them, I would score, but if I did not, I would walk away. I loved women who could hold conversations about anything, but then these were usually the same women who would walk away after they figured out what I wanted.

The fall of my senior year, everything I had learned in my junior high hygiene class became useful. My friends and I met a bunch of girls, and for some reason, all of them gravitated toward me. By coincidence, one of them was in my night-school class. We often hung out in Brooklyn's Prospect Park, drinking cheap wine and making out. At times, we would switch girls. We did not mind switching, because there was no commitment. The girls didn't mind either. All of us were interested in just one thing: having fun. A few months later, all of the girls joined the military, and I never saw them again.

◆ ◆ ◆

My first and only experience with the New York City police was after a hooky party. (A hooky party is when a group of kids cut class together and hang out.) At this particular event, Patrick and I had seven or eight girls cut class and party with us at a friend's house while his parents were at work.

The car I drove to the party belonged to a friend who still went to Wingate. He agreed to let me use it if I picked him up after school to take him to work. When it came time to leave, however, I realized that the girls who had partied with us were all so nice, I could not tell them to walk home. So I offered them all a ride.

On the way to the first house, just as I made a turn onto Utica Avenue, I heard a siren behind us. I pulled over. The police officer asked me for my license and registration. I gave him the registration, but told him I did not have a license. When the police officer discovered the car was not mine, he ordered the girls out. I explained to him that my friend had let me use the car for a hooky party and that I was just dropping these girls off before I picked him up for work at 2:15.

The two officers decided to take me to George Wingate High School. One of them drove me in the police car, and the other drove my friend's car. We made it just as my friend was coming out. My friend walked to his car and saw a police officer inside. The two then came over to the police car where I was waiting with the other officer. The officers gave my friend his keys and then drove me in the police car over to the basketball courts, where they parked.

I was worried. I had heard stories about getting arrested, and I didn't know who I would call if it were to happen to me. But they didn't arrest me. Instead, they just talked to me and tried to help me realize what I had done wrong. Sensing that I was not in big trouble, I relaxed, and the glove compartment caught my eye; on it were pictures of a bunch of well-endowed, half-naked women. I smiled. The two officers were players like me. Plus, I think they noticed my honesty. Finally, one of the officers said he would just write me a ticket so my parents would know about the incident and so I would think twice before I tried it again.

By the time I got home, however, Hernst was already at the Seventy-first Precinct looking for me. Hernst's friend had told him he'd seen the police take me in their car; little did he know we were going to Wingate and not to the precinct.

When Hernst got back, he told me how lucky I was, because my mother had just about called my father at work to tell him I was in jail. And then later that weekend, I went to the local pool hall, where word had spread that I had been arrested. The real crooks, now thinking I was cool, told me all about their experiences getting arrested. After listening to them, I felt lucky indeed.

◆ ◆ ◆

I was grateful to Hernst. I could not have taken so many classes in such a short period of time had he not let me use his car from September until January to do so. And so it happened that one day that winter, I asked my father to take the night off because I needed a ride to my high school graduation. He was pleasantly surprised. I graduated in the January class of 1973.

Chapter 5

When it came to choosing a career, I was divided. I wanted to play professional soccer, and my parents wanted me to find a job or go to college. Although I had graduated a semester early, my grades had been pretty poor, so the prospect of going to college seemed dim. On the other hand, I had an athletic scholarship to Ulster County Community College, ever since the coach had come into the city and recruited me.

I did not know anything about going to college; I knew only that it was something I had to do if I wanted a good-paying job. And since Hernst and most of my friends were already in college, I figured now it was time for me. I had to wait about seven months before the next semester started, however. So in the meantime, I went to several employment agencies. Not much later, I ended up in Dunn and Bradstreet's mailroom as a clerk.

I liked working there. Over lunch breaks, my coworkers and I would hang out down the street, watching construction on the Twin Towers, in disbelief at the heights of these workers, and in amazement that none of them ever fell.

During short breaks, I played touch football in the lobby with a guy we called only Tiny, who was about my age.

If I hadn't wanted to play soccer with UCCC so much, I could have landed a career with Dunn and Bradstreet. I could have taken advantage of its tuition-reimbursement program, enrolled in night school while working the day shift, and pursued a job-related degree. Eventually, my training would probably move me from the mailroom to a more attractive, better-paid position.

At that time, however, I hoped to land myself on a professional soccer team, which was only possible if I took the opportunity being handed to me to play for UCCC. So after several months at Dunn and Bradstreet, I resigned and went to college. I left a job with lots of opportunity to play a sport that most people not only had no clue about but also felt had no real future. To Tiny and the others I worked with, my dream would remain a dream, because they understood how very difficult it was to make it as a soccer player in America. They thought I was crazy for leaving Dunn and Bradstreet, a company where an entry-level position in the mailroom could lead to a lifetime career. I could have even replaced the Irish guy who was then retiring after many years of service.

My father, too, was against my attending UCCC, since it was all the way in upstate New York. He told me there were plenty of schools in New York City that I could attend. Take, for example, the City University of New York, where, my father said, I could join my brother.

◆   ◆   ◆

UCCC started in the summer with a pre-season practice, after which we were taken on a half-an-hour ride to New Paltz University, where we were paired with a roommate for the semester. (Because UCCC did not provide living quarters for its students, we all lived in the New Paltz dormitories). I was paired with a guy I didn't know, whose name was Jimmy. Jimmy didn't play soccer; in fact, he was a serious student. A few years older than I, he was also more mature.

The experience of dorm living would have been wonderful had I been ready for it. My dad even purchased me a used car to make my daily commute from New Paltz to UCCC easier. But I did not yet have the skills to live by myself.

Fortunately for me, I wasn't the only one struggling. It seemed all of the young adults around me were trying to find themselves.

Together, we made up a bunch of crazy, confused kids, though clearly, some were more confused than others.

Case in point: I remember once, when a bunch of us were outside Shango Hall talking, this naked guy ran by us, holding his penis. Then, before we could even say anything, another naked guy ran past, but holding his hands in the air. We all looked at one another, not knowing what to think except that those guys must have been crazy.

By the time we walked into our dorm room, we were laughing hysterically. A guy who had lived there several years asked us what we were laughing about, so we told him. He then explained to us that some fraternities required their new members to streak around campus as an initiation. Most of us had never seen such a thing. We soon became accustomed to it, however, because for the next few days, there were a lot of initiations taking place.

Living in Shango Hall was my first experience outside my parents' house. Shango was one of the older dormitories at New Paltz University, and it was predominately African American, with a few Spanish guys, and even fewer Europeans. It was the first time I really began to notice the difference between me and some of the other students that lived there. There was an overwhelming support among the serious students. These students, who were usually in four-year programs, had goals much different from mine; they would study together for all hours of the day. After time, however, I learned that some of these students were a few years older than I was, and they had gone through what I was experiencing now.

With that in mind, I had new hope for myself, and tried to get my bearings academically. And when it came time to register for the fall semester, I told the counselor who was helping me that I wanted to become a CPA. You see, at Dunn and Bradstreet, I had been impressed with one particular department, so one day I'd asked one of the guys in that department what he did. He'd said he was a certified public accountant.

As a result, the counselor gave me classes I could not handle. If the college had giving me an entrance exam, she would have known to give me only remedial classes, but because I was an athlete, I had been exempt from that exam. So I, the guy who had barely graduated from high school, was allowed to register for classes that I had no business taking. I tried hard in my classes, but my mind just wasn't cut out for studying; it was geared to play soccer.

At the same time, however, I was also losing points with the rest of my soccer team. And this is what led to my getting busted by the coach, who happened to make a surprise visit to my dorm room at the exact moment I was partying with a bunch of girls, some of whom were smoking joints.

The "funny" thing about that visit, which I did not learn until much later—after the season was over—was that everyone else on the team had known the coach was coming to visit. You see, the coach had liked me so much that he had been building the team around me, and this disappointed some of the other players. So one of them had set up the visit.

At the point I found that out, however, it no longer mattered to me. By then, I was just concentrating on what to do with my future, because by the final pre-season game, I had been cut from the team. For the second time in my life, I was rejected from playing soccer not because of my talent, but because of my ignorance.

◆ ◆ ◆

It was at this point that I began to see the reality of my situation. All along, I had been comparing the lifestyles of professional soccer players in Europe and South America to those of professional baseball or basketball players in America—players who made millions of dollars and retired by their mid-thirties. That was not the reality in the 1970s for U. S. soccer players.

So I continued my classes at UCCC, even after the engine on my car died. I had no money to fix it or buy a new car, so I had to catch a ride or hitchhike to school. My grades were not good. My highest grade that semester was a C, and that was in another sport—boxing.

I had registered for the class out of curiosity, because it was taught by Floyd Patterson, a former professional boxer who moved to the Ulster County area after his retirement in 1972. Floyd had a record of 55-8-1, and when I boxed with him in class, he told me I had a good right hand. So when I received a C in his class, I felt dejected. Even though it was my best grade, I knew deep down that I could have done much better.

Many students were interested in helping me, but I was not ready for their help. Once, a graduate student invited me to her off-campus apartment for just such a purpose, although, at the time, I thought it was a guise for her wanting to have sex.

So as soon as I saw her that evening, I experienced a painful erection, and I told her I did not come to get help but to make out. She told me that she was married, that it would not be cool, and that she had really just wanted to help me with school. I tried to read her expression, but I couldn't tell whether she was bluffing or playing hard to get. So I tested her a bit.

"Maybe another time," I said. "But right now, I want to get down." I then took out the condom I had brought with me from my back pocket and showed it to her.

She raised her eyebrows at me at laughed. I took her laughter to mean she wanted me, so I bent down, picked her up, and started to carry her toward the bedroom. She was petite and quite attractive, so the terrified look that crossed her face spoke volumes. I acquiesced and gently put her down, after which she quietly thanked me. I apologized, and then walked out of her apartment, ashamed and cursing myself.

It was at that point when I began examining the situation I had put myself into. On some level, I knew what I had to do, but it wasn't until one day, sitting in my dorm room and watching Jimmy hard at study, that I saw exactly what I needed to. Jimmy did not want to be around me, because I was a disturbance to his goals. He was here for a different reason: because he understood that he needed an education. And this is what confirmed my decision to leave UCCC.

When I told Jimmy I was not coming back, I saw relief in his face, which then changed to sympathy. He revealed who had set up the coach's surprise visit and confirmed that it was done intentionally to bust me because I had been getting too much attention on the team. He told me he regretted that the situation turned out so ugly, and wished things could be different.

I disclosed to him that even though I knew soccer was a team sport, I believed that the team had ended the season unsuccessfully because I had not played; I truly felt that if I had played, I could have made a difference. I also told Jimmy I was preparing to try out with teams in the North American Soccer League.

That was the most we ever said to each other, our entire time as roommates. But that conversation with Jimmy, and later conversations I was to have with other players, built my ego and made me more confident about my abilities in the long run.

Later that day, I went to the athletic director at UCCC and told him I needed some time off. He tried to stop me; he told me that I would have a better future here in school, that most people who took breaks never returned, and that he wanted me to reconsider my decision. I just continued to say, "I am not quitting. I just need time off."

When I returned to Shango Hall, I had my first and only piece of mail from my parents. I opened the envelope to find another envelope addressed to me at my parents' address in Brooklyn. I opened the second envelope and there was a letter inside. It was from Renee.

◆ ◆ ◆

Renee was an attractive African American woman I'd met at a club the summer before leaving for UCCC. The club was brand new, and Patrick and I had decided to go party there before he had to leave to join the army.

Renee and I talked the entire night. I lied to her about my age, which I did with most women I met, but Renee was mature, well-developed, and older. She had a car and an apartment, and had been working for a while in her government job. She lived in Baltimore, but by the end of the night, we were exchanging numbers, and we decided to see each other next time she came to Brooklyn.

Since her job gave her plenty of paid time off, she was able to visit twice. The first time, I took her to the West Indian Festival, where we followed a band from Utica Avenue to Grand Avenue Plaza, talking about my plans for the future: my dream of becoming a millionaire and retiring in my mid-thirties.

In the letter I now held in my hand, she gave me a number to call. I dialed it almost immediately, and after our conversation, the following week she drove from Baltimore to upstate New York to see me. My roommate, along with everyone else in the dormitory, was surprised to see this stylish, attractive girl pull up in a new car.

That weekend that Renee stayed with me was the best weekend. I wanted to show her off to the whole world. We drove around Ulster County, and I told her about my decision to leave school and try out for the North American Soccer League. She suggested I move to Baltimore with her. When we returned to the dorm, I kicked Jimmy out of the room, and Renee and I made love.

I could tell Renee really wanted to be with me, but, after being together, I was not sure I had satisfied her; I had spilled the wine a few times. She never complained. In fact, she said I blew her mind. But something about her made me want to learn how to truly make her happy in bed. I even asked advice of people I thought were more experienced than me: particularly, guys in long-term relationships.

After Renee's visit, it was definite that I would leave UCCC to pursue my professional soccer dreams. So I returned to Brooklyn, while she returned to Baltimore to prepare her apartment for the both of us.

While in Brooklyn at my parents' house, I got in touch with my friends from Victory, and immediately rejoined the team. It felt like I had never left. Then before I moved, Renee drove to Brooklyn to visit me a final time. That evening when she came in, we drove to Prospect Park, parked, and just sat talking until early morning. I did not pursue any other women after that. I really wanted to have a good relationship with Renee.

Chapter 6

In Baltimore, to my pleasant surprise, I received an invitation to try out for the New York Cosmos, the franchise that played soccer in New York. While in Brooklyn, I had sent a letter to them, but I hadn't expected to get a response. It was a dream come true.

The goal of this tryout was to find a local player for the team, because the colleges were not producing enough of them. So when the day came, I was not the only local player there. We were instructed to gather in a group and write down the positions we were accustomed to playing. And since we had enough players, the coaching staff then divided us into two groups, and we played against each other in a scrimmage.

After that, the coach selected some of us to play another game. My hopes were high when I was asked to play the second game as the right back. Unfortunately, I was not asked to return for a third scrimmage. Coach George Bradley spoke to me and a few other players, however, and told us not to give up. He said he wanted us to continue to play even though we had not been selected this time. He told us about the new vision the Cosmos had taken, which involved signing established players from all over the world, and said some of us probably had a better chance trying out with other upcoming teams who were not heading in this direction.

And so my desire grew, and I decided to try out for the Baltimore Comets. After playing right back for many years, I had the opportunity during the Baltimore tryouts to play center back. The other center back was an older international player from England, who took pride in my game, and taught me many strategies of the position. Although I did not make the team, I came out of tryouts a better and more versatile player.

Still, that left me in Baltimore with only a high school diploma, being supported by Renee, who was, fortunately, established in her job. I would just stay in the apartment all day, leaving only to pick up Renee from work.

Not surprisingly, Renee and I began to argue about my inability to support myself, so I went to this place in downtown Baltimore that offered on-the-spot job placement for unskilled labor. It was humiliating to think that in a matter of days, I could be mopping someone's floor or washing someone's car for a couple of measly dollars. Unfortunately, I didn't get in that day, so I had to return. The next day, a man called my name and asked me what I could do. He then told me about a job opportunity, but he talked so fast, I could not understand what he was saying, so I just responded with an "okay."

I ended up on the back of a sanitation truck. At first, it was cool. I pictured stopping at the corner store on the way home to pick up bread, milk, and eggs; showing up at Renee's afterward with a couple of dollars still in my pocket; and then making her breakfast the next morning to show my appreciation for her helping me.

But after being at it for few hours, my pride started to take over. The driver—the man in charge—was this young guy with long hair, who acted like the sanitation truck was his life. Meanwhile, I was standing on the back, holding on for dear life. Whenever we stopped, it was only long enough for me to pick up the garbage.

I began to notice the people passing us by. One time, a car honked behind me, in a hurry to pass. I looked back to see a new Volvo, driven by a woman who was well-dressed and well-groomed. Finally, as she passed us, she slowed down and stared at me. When I ignored her, she moved on.

Later, my own driver asked me, "Are you okay?" Apparently, he'd noticed that my demeanor had changed for the worse after picking up so many garbage cans.

"No, I'm not okay," I told him. "Where is the nearest public bus station, and how do I get back?"

He told me, though he seemed surprised that I did not also ask to be paid for the hours I had worked. I didn't want the money. My parents had not brought me to America to ride the back of a sanitation truck, especially at the rate they were paying. I did, however, get something from my few hours behind that sanitation truck: yet another eye-opener to reality.

When Renee got home that night, I told her how my day had gone. She was sympathetic with me. We talked about the area I had picked up trash in—an upper-class neighborhood with well-manicured lawns and picket fences—and Renee said she had friends there and that we could move there after I got the job I wanted.

Instead, I decided to return to New York.

◆ ◆ ◆

Since Victory had been established in the late sixties, we, the nucleus of the team— Errol, Perry, Harry, and I—remained close friends. Perry was the oldest, Errol and Harry about the same age, and I the youngest.

So when I moved back to New York, it was a given that I would immediately rejoin the team, which was in full force during the summer. We met at least twice a week for practice, and our rival teams were *Les As* from Manhattan and *Les Piquets* from Queens. We always had paying fans, but I did not get paid to play, and for me, it was not about the money anyway. For me, it was about the ambiance of the game and the interaction with the community.

After games, we'd gather in Errol's parents' basement, as we had done when we were younger, listening to music and drinking beer. We would also spend time at Junior's house listening to his record collection. Junior Lightburn, who had become the coach after Charlie had resigned, was older, had an established career as a dental technician, and was married and had five kids. I considered him our mentor in many areas, both off and on the field.

When I introduced Junior and my other friends to Renee, they were happy for me. They said they felt she had introduced some kind of stability into my young, confused life.

On one particular Sunday afternoon, in the summer of 1976, we were all ready to play at Boys High School in Brooklyn. We were playing *Les As*, which had many Haitian international players; Victory, on the other hand, consisted of younger players who had played the game mostly in America. This was a final game, which usually drew at least six thousand spectators, and many of our local fans had anticipated a win from us.

At one point during the first ten minutes of the game, playing my usual right back position, I tried to play back the ball to our goalie. Our goalie and I had made similar plays before; usually we were as one unit on the field, understanding and anticipating each other's plays. This time, however, he did not see me coming. He left the goal area, just as the ball rolled his way. I watched in horror as the ball slowly rolled to the back of our net. My teammates froze and looked at me. I had just scored a goal against my own team.

Les As fans were jumping and throwing kisses at me. I was shocked. I did not know what to say or do. So I just stood there for a moment.

For the rest of the game, we had many more opportunities to score, but we came up empty. We ended up losing the game to the one goal I had scored against my team. That goal had cost us the entire season. I was humiliated.

Chapter 7

Back home, I returned to the agency that had gotten me the job at Dunn and Bradstreet. I had liked that agency. When I got there, I read a sign in its window that said, "If you are not qualified for a job, lie." So I did. I put on my application that I was a few credits short of completing my degree in accounting.

This is how I landed a job in the accounting department at Phillip Brothers on Park Avenue, right next to the Waldorf Astoria. I was to work in account receivables as a clerk. Once I got my desk, however, it took me a full day to relearn how to sign my own name. And I could not seem to complete one sentence without making several grammar mistakes.

By the time my boss figured out that I was not close to having any degree, let alone an accounting one, however, he and all of my coworkers had grown to like me. Luckily, my main job was simple: having employees sign off on invoices. If the invoices were correct, they signed them and I would take them to the accounting department, where the payment would be issued or received. The job required responsibilities in addition to that; however, once my boss discovered my little secret, he made this task the bulk of my job, so that I could stay. Though the job had become easy for me by then, it likely also became stressful to those in my department, who had expected me to have more knowledge in accounting.

Another task I was given was to pick up or deliver important documents at the end of the week. Because Phillip Brothers was a predominantly Jewish firm, no one wanted to travel on Fridays.

So late on Thursdays, or on Fridays, I would fly out of New York or make trips to the New York Stock Exchange.

Lunchtime at Phillip Brothers was the best. We'd all sit on Park Avenue, watching the many celebrities who passed us by. At any time, you could catch one of them exiting a taxi in front of the Waldorf Astoria, where they would commonly stay while in New York.

On paydays, I would catch a cab myself, go to one of the discos that was open for lunch, and make it back before the big bosses returned from one of the famous French restaurants they frequented.

Similar to the experience I'd had at Dunn and Bradstreet, I could have used the tuition reimbursement program offered by the company to get a higher degree. By then, the job had paid enough for me to get my own apartment and a sense of being more mature, which, together, formed a foundation that I could build a career on. But I was not satisfied with the idea of staying at Phillip Brothers forever, so I decided to return to school. I resigned from my position in accounting, transferred my apartment lease to Hernst, and moved back into my parents' house.

Moving back into my parents' had restrictions—I had to stay in the small room that my brother and I had shared before he'd left and gotten married, and I could not host wild parties anymore—but deep down, I did not want to live that life anymore. I was tired of rolling joints, making sure there was beer in the fridge, and all of the other things that came with being a bachelor. Besides, the restrictions of living with my parents were far better than those of living alone—having the stress of paying the monthly rent and bills. I continued to work, however. I always had a job to maintain myself.

About the same time, Renee and I began to grow apart, because she wanted a more committed relationship, but I was not ready. She did not expect a commitment from me, but she transferred her job from Baltimore to New York, got an apartment nearby, and gave me time to think. If Renee and I had stayed together, I have no doubt that our relationship would have reached the next level. However, our timing was off; she wanted to commit to a way of life, when I was ready to commit to pursuing a dream, regardless of what was in front of me.

◆ ◆ ◆

I ended up at Brooklyn College as a non-matriculated student wanting to achieve academically. I registered for twelve credits of history, which included African, Puerto Rican, and world history. I met many friends, especially in the African history class. The professor of that class was a native African, and he introduced me to the Zulu tribe, Shaka, and Nelson Mandela. For the first time, I really began to understand the struggle that came from being of African origin in the United States; a struggle that had started several generations before my existence. As a result, I gained more respect for myself and for the history of my people.

Although I took it upon myself to improve in school, the temptation of becoming a professional soccer player still loomed. So instead of registering for extra help, I spent my time in the gym. And I ended the semester with incompletes in every class, because I did not take any of the final exams. But I did not end the semester without learning much. I learned that I still could not write. I learned to become resilient to failure, now that I had failed so many times. And I learned that regardless of color, people would treat you based on what benefits them.

I took the little money I had saved, and ended up on a plane to Dallas, to try out for the Dallas Tornados. And because my parents supported me only as long as I was in Brooklyn, I now officially had no one.

I was not accepted into the Dallas Tornados, but while trying out for them, an older gentleman saw me play and, afterwards, asked me to join his team, which played in the Dallas area. I accepted.

Still, it would not be until years later that I would finally realize that my dream of becoming a pro soccer player was only a dream. That professional sports is a business. That it is about making money. And that to succeed at it, you either have to be talented or extremely lucky or both.

In time, I would find out that I was neither. And in that time, I would learn the ins and outs of becoming a man.

◆ ◆ ◆

Meanwhile, in Dallas, I became like the character that John Travolta played in *Saturday Night Fever*. I was already slim, about six foot tall, and owned several three-piece suits and designer shirts. And now, every Saturday night, I either walked to the club with a woman on each arm or walked out of the club with the same. My club of choice was *Le Jardin*. It was not a heavy charge to get in, and if you looked and smelled good, it was automatic entry. It was also the disco that most of the Dallas Cowboys hung out at.

I was among the cream of the crop at *Le Jardin,* even among the famous football players. The club was a garden of beautiful women, not to mention the affluent who liked to dance, drink, and have a good time. I should have felt out of my league—even with its low cost, I had to save whenever I wanted to go, as I always liked to have a little extra for drinks. Conversely, the others' dollars just seemed to drop into the cash register each time a beautiful girl came to take their drink orders. But I did not feel out of place in the least. First, I was there so often that no one could tell me I did not belong. And, second, I truly believed it was something I had to experience to get where I wanted to be in life.

One night, one of the Cowboys' running backs—a Heisman Trophy winner—was watching me do my infamous Brooklyn disco moves. He was apparently envious, because I had the floor, not to mention four or five women dancing alongside me. These women had originally gotten on the floor to catch the attention of the football players, but had gotten mine instead. It did not matter to me though, because I was enjoying the moment. On the other hand, it was a great relief when the football players joined in and everyone was having an equally good time!

After everyone else sat down, one of the ladies, Linda, kept dancing with me. Then she asked me to have a drink with her. We started to talk, and she reminded me of Stephanie in *Saturday Night Fever*. She told me that there was no future in America for a professional soccer player and that I should stop talking uneducated Brooklyn English and go back to school before it was too late. I later found out that Linda was from Oklahoma and that she was not happy in her marriage.

After a while, she began to drive the couple hours' distance to come see me in Dallas. Although we had just met, it seemed that we had a connection with each other; we both had something missing in our lives. We would talk and share our deepest feelings. Her problems with her husband were not common to me, but I offered her an ear, and she was compassionate and sincere with me.

I always enjoyed being with Linda, but I was not always sure when she would visit. On several occasions when Linda came, I would have a game. On those times, she would wait for me outside my apartment, sometimes leaving a note on my door letting me know she had stopped by.

Other times, she would stand me up because she could not get away from her husband for the many hours it would require her to visit. On those times, I would wait for her, worrying, not knowing what had happened. But she would always find a way to call to let me know she was okay.

On one occasion, I visited her. I took the forty-five-minute shuttle to see her and flew back the same night to Dallas.

Whenever we did get together, though, our conversations were mostly about how inconsiderate and selfish her husband was and how I should not pursue soccer as a profession.

So it was not by choice that, on some nights when Linda came to see me, I had other female company—namely, Nancy. On those times, when I told Linda I had company, she would say, "It's okay, as long as she is only a friend. You didn't know I was coming." Then she would go back out to her car and wait for Nancy to leave. Usually, Nancy would not leave, Instead, she would tell me to tell Linda to go away. I never did, but Linda would get tired of waiting and leave anyway.

I had met Nancy by accident. She was a younger sister of someone else I had met, who had been in Dallas on vacation from New Orleans. Nancy was tall and cute, with a lean, athletic body. She was a few years younger than I was and very competitive; she would jog with me and finish the entire five-mile run. We would spend the weekend talking, giggling, and playing, and at night when no one was at the pool, we swam. Nancy did not know much about soccer and, unlike Linda, did not care whether I played, but she enjoyed the fact that I was trying to achieve at a professional sport. In our lonely times—because her family was in Louisiana and mine was in Brooklyn—we would show each other the most compassion. She would even sing me a song.

◆ ◆ ◆

And as destiny had it, lots of things began brewing in my favor. One of the coaches who had seen me play wanted to give me an opportunity to go to school. I tried out and was offered a full-ride scholarship at North Texas University in Denton. I was ecstatic. North Texas was in the first division and played the best college teams.

I began to prepare myself to return to school again, by looking at myself in the mirror. I loved to look at my physical body, but I had to question my inner self. *How would I fare on a television interview?* I thought. *Could I make myself proud or would I sound like a person who couldn't speak properly?* I spent days in front of the mirror, reading and spelling out words, and I realized that I did not meet my own standards. I became increasingly critical of myself, and realized that I needed to get back on track. I needed to work toward a goal that was *realistic* for me.

Incidentally, not much later, I met a radio announcer at *Le Jardin*. She had a Sunday show, and wanted to use an upcoming broadcast to interview me about soccer because the sport was new to her. I agreed to the interview, but after listening to the broadcast, realized that nothing I said was correct. I was not nearly as articulate as I wanted to be. Fortunately, my accent probably saved me from sounding like a total disgrace.

In that same time frame, Tony Dorsett, a first-round draft pick from Pittsburgh University, was a regular at the club. I looked up to him, because he was about my age and had accomplished in football what I had always wanted to accomplish in soccer. He looked and acted like a nice guy, too—a wealthy and healthy dude.

The same Sunday the radio station played my botched radio interview, he was on television. As I watched him, I learned that he was not only a great running back, but also an articulate twenty-three-year-old. No one else would ever compare me with Tony, but I did. I did not just see him as someone I wanted to be; I saw his strengths, and I wanted to gain those strengths, because they were my weaknesses: a college degree, success in sports, and the ability to conduct an interview on national television professionally. I could not even imagine attaining his athletic success, because it was so beyond mine, but I was happy for him and the other guys from the Dallas Cowboys who hung out at *Le Jardin*.

At the same time, I also noted that many of the guys now returning from the Vietnam War were coming back with some kind of addiction, most often to heroin. I counted myself lucky that I was not among those in the streets, either killing themselves or performing illegal activities for a fix. I felt fortunate to have been able to stay in a positive environment, where I would not be more tempted to fall into this other lifestyle that was, in fact, quite reachable.

Chapter 8

Before finding my own place in Dallas, I had stayed with my friend Gerry and his wife Maude. When I moved out, it was into an apartment in the same complex, so I still visited them often. In fact, I hung out at their place quite a bit, as it had become kind of my home away from home.

So when applying for jobs, I listed Gerry's phone number as well as mine. And one Sunday afternoon, while at Gerry's apartment, I got a call from a family-owned business called Love Field Entertaining Center. They set up an interview, after which they hired me to work in their box office as a manager. Finally at the end of seeking work in the North American Soccer League, it was a relief to me to find a real, paying job.

Soon after, on a Saturday afternoon, I sat on my couch, which faced the sliding door that overlooked the swimming pool. Everyone was out having a good time, and suddenly, I began to wonder about my future. For the first time, I began to wonder how it would have been to be born in America. And I wondered whether, if I had put in the effort and dedication that I had devoted to soccer all these years into another, more lucrative sport, I could have been more successful. I measured success in big homes, beautiful cars, and lots of money; those who were unsuccessful, I felt, were not good enough to enjoy that kind of life.

It became apparent that I was seeking something that did not exist. I was in the wrong place; the wrong country. That is, even though I was talented enough to get a professional contract, like the players in Europe and South America, I had no one to help me get there.

As I sat in my luxurious, air-conditioned studio apartment, overlooking the pool—a setting that, for some, would mean success—I wanted more. I wanted more than the two-story house that my parents had owned in Brooklyn. I wanted not to have to work as hard as my dad always had.

I remembered the time, recently, when I had stopped at a gas station, and across from me, using the same pump, was one of the Dallas Cowboys. Sitting comfortably in the passenger seat of his new, expensive car was a well-groomed, well-dressed, beautiful woman, glittering in all her jewelry. In the back of their convertible sat their beautiful young girl.

It caught me by surprise that they were looking at my old beat-up Ford, which needed oil as much as it needed gas. (The gasket had a leak, so every couple of days, I had to put oil in the car.) I guess I caught their attention because, despite what I was driving, I was wearing my suit, a white-collar shirt, and a belt and tie that matched my shoes; I had been on my way to work. The irony of the situation caught me. On one side of the gas pump was America's success, and on the other an immigrant struggling just to make it.

As I sat watching the pool-goers, however, I noted that these wealthy others were human too—just like me.

I jumped when the phone rang; it was my mother. I laughed, happy to hear from her, and greeted her in our Haitian Creole language. For fifteen minutes, we talked, and she informed me that my friend Irene had called and wanted to know my number. My mother sounded unhappy and concerned when I told her I was starting school at North Texas in September, and that I wanted to come home to see her before then.

As soon as I hung up the phone with my mother, Irene called. We spoke for a long time, and she was full of encouragement. I was very selfish, but she allowed me to be because she knew I was lost. She showed interest in coming to see me in Dallas, because someone she knew had recently moved there.

Not wanting Irene to see me just barely making it, I played off her visit. I had pride. I could not tell her that I was driving an old beat-up Ford that leaked oil, which I did not have money to fix. I could not tell her that was living off TV dinners and working as box office personnel at Love Field Entertaining Center. Granted, Love Field was doing well, but I realized in hindsight that I was likely hired because I was probably the only black man willing to wear a suit for such low wages; the check barely paid for my studio apartment.

If I was broke, it was my business. Irene did not need to know. Besides, I knew that in the coming weeks, before fall semester started, I would be travelling to see my parents. So, I told Irene that we would talk once I got to New York.

Chapter 9

I had met Irene when I lived in my apartment in Brooklyn, around the time Renee and I were parting ways and I was about to resign from Phillip Brothers.

My friend Jimmy, who painted the centerpiece of an Earth Wind and Fire album on my living room wall as a backdrop for all of my wild disco parties, was a DJ at a club in downtown Brooklyn. We hung out at the club a lot, and I basically had a free pass to get in any time.

One night, however, when I arrived at the club, a lady asked me for the entrance fee. I looked at her as if she were crazy. She said there was a private party, so everyone had to pay to get in. I don't remember paying, but I ended up inside and having a good time.

The club was set up with the dance floor on one side, and the game and conversation room on the other. On this night, I ended up on the games-and-food side and sat down. I smelled the aroma of fried chicken, macaroni and cheese, beef ribs, and sweetened iced tea coming from a buffet table, so I grabbed a plate and proceeded to help myself. When I went back for seconds, I realized that the others in line were paying. So I approached the woman behind the counter and mentioned that I had inadvertently eaten for free. I told her, however, that I did not have the money to pay for what I had eaten, so I wanted to try to ameliorate the situation.

She looked up and said it was okay, but I told her that, on her break, she could come over and I would make it up to her by teaching her to play chess—even though I was not very good. She accepted.

When the time came, I pulled her chair close enough that we could hear each other. I decided that I would not start by asking her for her sign. That would show that I was a player. Instead, I said, "I did not get your name."

"You did not get it, because I did not give it to you," she said.

This is going to be a hard nut to crack, I thought, but then I smiled and whispered to myself, "I like it that way."

And this was how I met Irene.

I was lucky I knew much more about chess than Irene. I showed her how the pieces moved around the chess board and, in particular, how the king could only move one step in any direction and the queen could move as she pleased, and how to knock the king off his throne. I would have liked to knock her a little, but I kept my cool and worked on a friendship—that is what it seemed like she wanted. She was so happy with every little move I showed her. She'd respond with things like "Oh, wow!" followed by genuine laughter.

We talked the entire night. I found out that the party was for her older sister Dorita's birthday and that they were charging because they wanted to get their money back for their expenses.

I usually waited for Jimmy to finish spinning and put his albums away, after which we'd catch the Number Three Train to Foster Avenue. But tonight, when it was time to close, I helped Irene load her car—a brown Dodge. When Jimmy saw I was busy, I winked at him, and he left to catch the subway home.

After everything was cleaned up and closed down, I sat in Irene's passenger seat, and we continued talking. I learned that she worked, went to nursing school, and was studying for her Registered Nursing Board exam. As we exchanged numbers, I thought it would be too much to ask her for a ride home. But on the train, on my way home, I replayed every single moment of our night.

Chapter 10

It was time to make my move and be successful. I wanted to improve myself. I wanted to learn and to sharpen the skills that would give me a better life. I did not want to be around anything that would *not* be about my going back to school.

As such, I began to prepare myself for school that September, writing and reading every chance I had. I planned my flight to Brooklyn to see my parents and to give them the good news that I had planned to graduate in Dallas and then to stay there to find my bearings. I wanted to make them proud, because this was what they had always wanted for me. I wanted them to know that I had finally gotten the message that school was important, that my tuition and book payments would be taken care of, and that I would play at a first-division school. I wanted them to know that, with the help of my recruiters, I was able to find an off-campus apartment, an academic program that I could cope with, and a job that would help me with my additional expenses.

My recruiter was against my going to Brooklyn. He wanted me to stay and prepare for school, and to participate in summer camp, where I would train with the team and get accustomed to their style of playing. He also wanted me to be there to set an example, since all of the other recruits were younger. Most had just graduated from high school, and had a different perspective about college. But when I told him that I was going to New York because I wanted to see my mother, he reluctantly agreed.

◆ ◆ ◆

My friend Perry picked me up at La Guardia Airport, and drove me to my parents' house on East Ninety-fourth Street. When I got there, Mom did not look good. She was pale and appeared weak, and she told me she had not been feeling well. I decided we should take a cab to Kings County Hospital Emergency Room.

Kings County was always crowded, as it served a huge area of Brooklyn, so we had quite a wait in the ER. In the time we were there, my mom became weaker and then eventually passed out on the floor. I tried to pick her up, but I could not. Finally, a nurse came to help me, and we immediately got her to the examining room and got her treatment. It was only the flu; however, later, she told me that she had been diagnosed with cervical cancer and thought that had been the reason for her severe weakness.

Later that day, I drove my dad's car to the public library at Grand Avenue Plaza, to do some research on cancer. It was at that point I became scared about my mom's health. I read that cancer was a disease in which, for some reason, your good cells stop functioning and do not mature properly; that is, they do not operate as normal cells. These immature cells start to multiply and form their own network, and then, with the help of the blood supply, spread to other parts of the body. As they continue to spread and grow, these immature cells form growths all over the body, which stops the normal activity that the body needs to survive. The body then starves, and the toxin produced by the immature cells poisons the body. People have many different cells in their bodies, and every one of them has the ability to turn cancerous. In addition, cancer can go for many years before it is detected.

◆ ◆ ◆

My mom told me that Irene had kept in touch with her while I had been away. All of my friends who were significant in my life—Irene was no exception—met my mom, talked on the phone with her during my time in Dallas, and, as it turned out, were there on my return. Irene called me minutes after she knew I was back in Brooklyn, which happened to be right after our return from the hospital, and she told me that she wanted to come over.

Her timing was perfect. I did not think that my mom would die, but I was shocked, and I wanted to find her help, and I didn't know what to do or who to turn to. And in an instant, Irene was there.

We caught up a bit, and I learned that Irene had graduated, passed her exam, and was now working at a hospital near my mother's house. Then I told her that I had just taken my mother to the emergency room at Kings County and did not like the slow service that resulted from it being too crowded. I told Irene that I was determined to help my mom, because, in my eyes, I felt that she was asking me for help.

After we hung up, Irene came over immediately and took my mother to the emergency room at the hospital where she worked—Kingsbrook Jewish Hospital—to get another opinion of my mom's condition. My mom was admitted promptly, and tests revealed she had grade four cancer of the cervix.

The doctors told my mom she had to be operated on, or she would soon die. But they also came to the decision that the intricacy of such an operation, caused by the fact that the cancer was so far along, required a specialist. They referred her to a surgeon at the Women's Hospital in Midtown Manhattan.

By the time we got home, Mom had made up her mind to have the operation. And so, Irene by her side, my mom left again and signed herself up at the hospital.

When my father found out where she was and what she was doing, he showed up at the hospital and went so ballistic on the doctors, they had to call hospital security to calm him down. My father thought he was defending my mom by interjecting with the procedure, because, like many others, he believed that some doctors operate on patients for no reason but to make money.

He was fighting because he did not want this to happen to my mom.

Later, Hernst told me that soon after they had arrived in America, when our mom was in her mid-thirties, a doctor wanted to do a biopsy because he thought he saw an abnormality. But my dad prevented it, because he thought his wife was too young and he did not believe the doctor anyway; he though the doctor wanted to explore and earn money while doing so. In his own way, my dad was protecting her.

There were other times, too. He had taken her to other institutions, because she had had profuse and excessive bleeding, and needed a medical procedure to determine the cause. All of those institution gave the same diagnosis, but my father chose not to further investigate her problem. My dad and many others in our community didn't have full confidence in the medical field; they believed that because they were not wealthy, they were given doctors who could make things worse.

From one perspective, this all sounded awful to me. But looking back at it, I had no doubt that his love for her was the determining factor of his delaying her operation. It was fortunate that my mom and the doctor at the Women's Hospital convinced my dad that the operation was the right decision. In the end, that decision would prove to have saved Mom's life.

It was a tough time in our household.

First, my mom had to undergo an operation that most people feared. I was very confident she would make it, however, because I did not know any better, and I could not even think about losing my mother. I was so self-centered at the time, wanting to prevent my own grief, that I did not even fully understand her prognosis. I did not realize that there was a high mortality rate among those diagnosed with cervical cancer.

Because my mom was already in stage four, the doctors had to remove her uterus and bladder, so the cancer would not spread to those organs. They also put in an implant, so she could undergo radiation after her chemotherapy had ended.

After her operation, my dad never verbalized to me how he felt. He was always with her, though, and gave her all of the care she needed to recuperate. And I felt that he was more relaxed now that the ordeal was at least under control. He remained there with her, and with us, through it all, and continued to provide for his household.

The whole family participated in helping her. We took her to get her chemotherapy and made sure she took all of her treatments. My younger sister Martina was exceptionally active, even taking off a year of school to take care of her. I helped with what I could, and spoke to my mom on a regular basis whenever I could not be at home.

My mother memorized many Bible verses during this time, which she would recite in French. And she would use all of the homeopathic medicine she was accustomed to, to ameliorate the effects of the chemotherapy and, later, the radiation.

Irene, too, would help. During lunch breaks and after work, she would come to the house to see just my mom and nurse her; there were times I did not even know she was there.

As my mom got stronger, Irene started coming by when she knew I would be home. She would come to my room for a while, and we would talk about current events, sports, music, and past relationships. It was somewhere during these conversations that we started to look at each other in a different way. I felt that, in Irene, I had a friend who heard me and understood where I was coming from. To me, it was confusing, but she saw a future in my confusion.

Chapter 11

Just before I was to return to Dallas, I sustained an injury playing a Victory game. My friends hoisted me into someone's car and drove me to the nearest hospital. An x-ray showed that I had a straight fracture in my right tibia.

I was devastated. I thought, *There goes my scholarship at North Texas.* I knew that camp had already started, and I didn't have six to eight weeks for my foot to heal. I called my recruiter and told him that I had an injury and would not be able to play this season. There was nothing either one of us could do, so the conservation ended with a solemn "Good luck to you." And since I couldn't play soccer for them, which was the whole reason I'd gotten the scholarship, I did not return to Texas for classes, either.

Over the next few weeks, one of my mom's neighbors, who was a pastor, came on several occasions to pray for me. He would touch my cast and read scripture and wish to God that my leg would get better so that I could continue my journey. He told me, "It is not over; it is just the beginning. God will give Arnaud the strength."

Irene would stop by too, usually for lunch, but also sometimes after work on her way to St. Albans Queens.

Lying in my bed all that time, I realized that even though I wanted more, not only from Irene but also from life, I should be grateful for what I had. I had had the opportunity to be among the rich. I had had two great career opportunities. I had gotten opportunities to better myself. But I also saw what my parents and others had been telling me for so long: without an education—and now an injury—where would I end up?

Many times, I passed the hours by watching the news. I could not help but be shocked at the drama that was going on in our community. There were many young, black men about my age coming back from Vietnam with only limited skills; they knew how to use violence and how to inject heroin into their veins. These guys were on the streets of most of the major cities in the United States, destroying themselves and their communities.

With few jobs left for these veterans, some committed crimes just to feed their families; others did it because of greed. Either way, I found it hard to believe that people would kill each other for money. I watched and learned, from the safety of my parents' house, how they were forming violent gangs, landing many young black men in jail or in funeral homes.

I began to feel thankful for my friends and family, because I knew that it was due to their influence that I had not—and would not—give in to that lifestyle; a lifestyle that led to the death and destruction I witnessed daily on the front pages of the newspapers.

At that point, after having been on my back for almost eight weeks, I also began to wonder, *If I had not had my parents or anyone else to help me, what would have happened to me?* I gained a great appreciation for all of the people I knew: my parents, in whose house I felt secure, because there was always food and warmth there, and the Victory guys—my gang—with whom I shared a common love of soccer.

As the time drew closer to having my cast removed from my leg, I began to realize that sports would no longer be an option for me. Though I did not know where I would end up, I knew it would not be as a professional soccer player. And I knew that, like everyone else who had dreams of becoming successful and rich, I would have to earn it. And even then, I would never become a millionaire.

After the cast came off, during my recuperation, the world slowed down and made me realize I was not even in the right lane. I was in a lane that was much too fast, and it was my overcharged ego that had gotten me there. I needed to take a deep breath and reexamine what I wanted to do for the rest of my life.

Irene helped me with this process. She and I had become closer than ever, when she gave me these words of encouragement: "God has something out there in store for you, and if it is not soccer, you have to find out what it is and how to go about getting it."

I knew she was right. At twenty-three years old, I still had determination and aspiration, and I knew I had to make a decision before it was too late.

I realized that in prior years, I had given up every other opportunity that came my way just to play soccer. I put all of life into one basket. And suddenly, it was no longer important whether I had money, fame, or luxury. What was important was life, and I needed to heal so that I could move on with mine. I did not give up prematurely like the guys in the streets did. I wanted to live and to give life to others.

Once I recovered, things returned to normal—at least on the outside; I saw my friends and went to parties, the way I always had. But on the inside, my eyes had opened beyond the parties and the drinking and the joint-rolling. They had opened beyond this little life in Brooklyn, and they had opened beyond myself.

My main concern at that point became my mom's well-being. The operation and the treatment had indeed extended her life, and for that, my family was very grateful. She was also getting stronger, despite the side effects from the chemotherapy and radiation. Still, I knew she would never return to the way she was before the operation. And because of that, I knew that I was home in Brooklyn for good, because I never wanted to leave her. I had been so self-centered before, traveling and not paying much consideration to her. Now I wanted to give her all of my attention. I had to make it up to her.

Chapter 12

After getting a job, I regularly visited Irene's two-bedroom apartment, where she lived with her son Salaam. I spent much of my weekends and other days off there. Not long after that, I moved in.

One evening, during the summer of 1978, we sat together on her comfortable burgundy sofa, watching television, when I realized, yet again, the fallacy of my belief that I could become a professional soccer player. And, thus, I started talking. I confessed everything to Irene. I told her about my womanizing days, and said that I was tired of that now, that I wanted to settle down and start a family. I also told her about my days at *Le Jardin*, how I'd felt so inferior to the Cowboys because I hadn't had a college degree or a professional sports team to play for. I told her that I had tried on many occasions to attend school, but felt that I just could not attain a college degree like I wanted.

Irene was always a good listener, and now she just sat and let me share my feelings without judging me. She helped me realize that the guys at *Le Jardin* were the finished products of years of hard work and help from many people. Then she suggested that I start looking into a career in laboratory medicine.

I thought about a few doctors I knew from Haiti who worked in labs, and their lives were going well. They had homes, cars, and families. She thought it would be a good profession because I would have the weekends to play recreational soccer. I agreed. I knew I should at least try it.

A few days later, Irene brought me information about an eighteen-month laboratory technician program at a school in

Manhattan. I went there, inquired about the school, and met with a financial advisor. By the end of the summer, I was registered to enter the program at Mandl.

After recovering from my broken tibia and accepting the fact that my playing ball from now on would be only recreational, I had my best summer season ever with Victory. I enjoyed playing with my friends, and our games had grown, as soccer had become increasingly popular. The high school field that we normally played at became too small—or, that is, its parking lot became too small. Fans began parking anywhere they could just to get to our games, even if it meant blocking streets and residential driveways. When the surrounding community began to complain, we had to move to bigger fields with bigger parking lots.

The good times I had with Harry, Perry, Serge, Errol, and Junior that summer were memories I would treasure forever. In particular, I enjoyed helping Harry, Perry's younger brother, practice, since he also played with the New Jersey Generals. We'd go to the beach to kick around the ball, and then we'd jog along the shore. Once, he even invited me to practice with the Generals, after which Harry told me the coach wanted to see me back.

"It's too late," I said to Harry. I told him that Irene and I were getting serious, and that I had already made up my mind to return to school and pursue a career in laboratory medicine. Harry gave me a look I had gotten countless times, from both him and others—the time I announced my decision to go to UCCC, the times I attempted to go to Baltimore and to Boston and to Dallas, and the time I tried to make it at Brooklyn College.

His look took me aback, and I began to second-guess myself, until I remembered. I remembered the roots of my decision. I remembered how horrible I'd felt lying on that bed, incapacitated because of a broken leg. I remembered how confused and without direction I'd felt. I remembered the many other athletes who had been injured and had nothing to fall on. These were the determining factors of my decision.

"I'm happy for you," I told Harry. "I am just not in that frame of mind anymore."

Chapter 13

That fall, I entered the medical technician program at Mandl School in Manhattan, next to Studio Fifty-four. Ready and eager, I walked up the steps to the second-floor classroom. There were so many of us that the people in charge had to divide our class of about fifty to seventy-five into two, to accommodate everyone. The fact that so many others were interested in the program, however, gave me a feeling of relief, a feeling that I was not alone in my endeavor.

The fact that about ninety-eight percent of the school was women would turn out to be a true test of my acknowledgement that my player days were over. These were very attractive women, too, even the teachers, which was what usually triggered my weakness; once I saw a beautiful woman, I couldn't help but start acting stupid. Though the students here had to wear uniforms, women included, it was a reminder to me of my days at *Le Jardin* and other clubs and parties.

The difference now, however, was that I was focused. I was focused on school and on Irene. So I decided to take class one day at a time and to try my hardest. And as I met many of the young women and realized how smart they were, I began to forget about acting stupid. I began to find it easier to limit my conversations with them to class-related discussions.

Within days, the class started to shrink as students discovered that either they were not ready for this program or that the program was not for them. And with each subsequent week, those who failed a certain number of tests would be disallowed to continue the program. After a month, only twenty-five students remained, three of whom were guys.

This selection process was necessary because after that first month, we really got into studying. We started with anatomy, physiology, hematology, chemistry, histology, blood banks, and microbiology. These classes were intense, and because I did not have prior knowledge in these subjects, they required that I spend many hours studying.

Though I had some of the same problems here that I had had at Brooklyn College and UCCC, at Mandl, I was able to prosper because of the hands-on portions of the classes; after we studied a topic, it would be presented in the laboratory. Another great help was that, although class went from 8 AM to 4 PM on Monday through Friday, the school was also open on Saturdays to provide students with extra help.

The combination of extra help, hands-on training, and my new personal incentive to land a career meant that, for the first time in my young life, I was able to focus. And my grades began to improve.

Each week, I had to get all of my school work done before Saturday, because I had a job on the weekends. I had been hired as a security guard for a company on Long Island. Working for them was perfect at the time, because the hours they offered fit into my schedule: twelve-hour shifts on Saturday and Sunday. It was not enough to pay all of the bills, but it was enough to contribute.

Irene primarily paid the bills. She worked as a registered nurse, and though her salary was better than mine, it alone could not support the three of us. We had a car note; an apartment; telephone, gas, and electric; food, of course; and private school for Salaam.

I also enjoyed working as a security guard because it afforded me extra time to study. Most of the time, I'd be given an off-site assignment, so I would drive to the location, take my hourly security walk inside so that management would note my presence, and stay in the car the rest of the time, studying. One time, when I went to pick up my check, the dispatcher told me there was a complaint about my reading on the job. I told her, "If there is a problem, send me someplace else, or deal with it."

I could say that because I had leverage at this company, and it was dependability. If there was ever a problem at a site or if they needed someone at the last minute to work late Friday night, they would call on me. So I continued working as a security guard for the entire eighteen months I was a student.

◆ ◆ ◆

Toward the end of the medical technician program at Mandl, we remaining students learned that we were required to do a six-month internship before we could be eligible to take the New York City medical technician examination. The catch: there were fewer internships available than there were students, and even once we were placed, we would receive no income.

That night over dinner, Irene and I discussed my future. I told her that I had become interested in science and wanted to pursue more than what Mandl had to offer. I was interested in going back to college to obtain a bachelor of science degree in medical technology. I wanted to do this because, as a technician, I would be limited to one department. I would either work in hematology, chemistry, blood banks, histology, or microbiology.

Irene was not immediately enthused by the idea. "These past months have been a challenge for us," she said, "because you are working this security job and going to school. And now you want to go on for another four years. Besides," she added, "I already found you an internship in the lab at the hospital."

I looked up at her, and she proceeded to tell me that she had already talked to the lab's supervisor. She said he had told her to get in touch once I was ready for my internship, and that they would help me pass the NYC technician exam.

I explained how I had always wanted to complete my bachelor of science degree and how most of the other students at Mandl already had higher degrees. I also assured her that, although it would take an additional four years to get my degree, I would work regardless, and that, in the long run, going further in school would benefit us as we prepared to raise a family.

Chapter 14

The next morning as I caught the Number Four Bus for my ride to Mandl, I had extra spring in my step. I knew that my conversation with Irene would soon set in and that she would realize continuing my education was the right thing to do. I was equally happy to learn that she had already talked to someone about my possibly interning at her hospital.

I did not mention this to any of my classmates, however, because it would have made them extremely jealous. To get an internship so quickly was the dream of every student in the program. Because in addition to the limited training positions available, the school had limited affiliations, so we were on our own to find internships after graduation.

As we neared the end of the program, the work became so intense that, to survive, we all had to depend on one another for help. Most of us were struggling and stressed on a daily basis, either finishing a project or worrying about the next test. Classes became increasingly smaller, which meant everyone saw their classmates' test grades—embarrassing for students who had failed or even done poorly.

That day, I decided to inquire about further education in the laboratory. I met with the counselor at Mandl, who, to my surprise, told me I was not the only student interested in continuing my education.

I learned that there were programs at nearby colleges that offered bachelor of science degrees in medical technology. The suggested route was to graduate, pass the exam, and get a full-time lab job during the day, using my nights to go to school to pursue my degree. I considered that option, but realized it would require me either to work for an employer who offered tuition reimbursement or to take out student loans. Although getting my degree was important to me, my main focus was still Irene's and my future as a family; I wanted to do whatever would work to make our relationship better.

On the train ride home, as always, I found a seat in the front and passed the forty-minute ride by studying—I would read the materials that were discussed in class that day, and try to understand the concepts or memorize the formulas. (On occasions when all of the front seats were taken, I would read standing up, holding the rail.)

From time to time, I'd be distracted from reading by the streets of Manhattan. Not only by its huge, million-dollar offices, its restaurants, and its wealthy, exciting night life, but also by its homeless people. It was a reminder of the contrasts of life. It was also a reminder to me that, though I had accepted that being rich was out of the question, I knew that going to school and planning a future was a sure thing that would help me eventually to provide for my family.

At the final stop, I caught Number Four, which again, I rode while reading. At one spot during the trip, however, I would look up from my book at a particular house that seemed always to catch my attention. The elderly owners had kept it up well. The wife had gray, well-maintained hair, and the husband was a slim, tall gentlemen. They always dressed nicely and kept the driveway filled with two of the same late-model vehicles. They sat and enjoyed summer afternoons on their porch. This was how I wanted to spend my later years with Irene.

That night at dinner, I echoed to Irene that it was important for me to go beyond Mandl. I was still not sure how we could afford it, but I felt if there were an opportunity somewhere, I would take it in an instant.

◆ ◆ ◆

When I moved in with Irene, we had seen it as kind of a trial marriage, to see if we could get along with each other, but also mostly if I could head a family. I had seen firsthand how my father had done it, but I had never tried it myself. The most important thing, I realized, was that I needed to maintain steady employment—and the only way to be able to do that successfully was to continue my education.

Over time, Irene and I talked more about the possibility of getting married, and as we did, we became concerned about Salaam's relationship with his father as well as his bond with me, which we formed as I helped him with his school work and as he hung out with me on Saturdays. We would often drop Salaam off at his father Van's apartment to spend the weekend, but this had become increasingly difficult, because there was not mutual financial cooperation between Irene and Van.

Eventually, Salaam, Irene, and I had decided that the best decision for our family after the marriage was to continue to follow the family court's decision that Salaam live with us.

As Irene and I dreamed about our future, we also reminisced about our past. One night, as the three of us sat in the living room watching television after dinner on a Friday night, I told Irene how I remembered meeting Salaam when he was a young, well-dressed boy of three. And now here we were together, just a few years later, living together and discussing marriage. Neither Irene nor I ever thought our relationship would mature this far.

When I had first met Irene, when she was still in nursing school, she had lived with her parents. Her two older sisters, Saddie and Dorita, had already been married, and Thomas and Joe, her brothers, had their own place together. Irene and her younger sister, Esther, were still living at home in St. Albans.

Irene was from a hard-working American family. Irene's father, Ernest Lenwood Wiggins, born in Norfolk, Virginia, in May 1917, worked for the city of New York and was the pastor of a church that he and his wife had founded. Irene's mom, Alma Lee Bachus, born in Colerain, North Carolina, in December 1917, was a housewife who ran the day-care center next to the church that helped pay for the church's expenses. Irene's parents had both left the South and met later in New York. Irene was born in Manhattan, where the Wiggins family had lived before landing in St. Albans Queens.

Irene had left home when she got pregnant, because her father had not been happy that she was having a baby without being married. Salaam's paternal grandmother was supportive and had let Irene live with her for a while. Irene later returned home, however, when her father had a change of heart, at which point, her parents helped her go back to school.

It was about that time when Irene and I started hanging out. We would go to my friends' houses. She would follow me in her car when I'd jog from my parents' house on East Ninety-fourth, all the way around Prospect Park, and then back to my parents' again. She drove with her nursing book on her lap and claimed to study at the stop lights. We took many trips to the botanical garden in Brooklyn, next to the Brooklyn Public Library, when the rose bushes and trees were in full bloom. We would walk in Prospect Park, holding hands as she'd tell me how her parents had gotten out of the projects of Harlem and moved to Queens in the 1960s, and how isolated and wooded the Queens area had been.

At first, my friends did not like Irene. My protective friends did not want me to get involved with someone who had a child. Regardless, we stood firm on our decision to be together.

There had been times in between then and now, when I would move away from Irene. She was never happy about our not being together, but she always gave me time to find myself and come back to her later.

In our relationship, we were friends first and became committed to each other after. Irene was about the only person I had allowed to get so close to me. I was exceedingly honest with her, telling her everything, and in doing so, building a sense of trust between us. And the camaraderie we shared continued even as we became closer.

Chapter 15

On an autumn afternoon in 1979, after my twenty-fifth birthday, I asked Irene to marry me. We were at Hempstead State Park having a barbeque, and I had my head on her lap as I usually did whenever we watched Salaam running around or riding his bike.

I felt I was ready to take on the responsibility of being a husband, father, and lifelong friend. I had no ring with me, but she did not expect anything; all of our expectations revolved around the future.

Irene replied the way she always did when she was surprised. "You deep man!" That was her way of saying, "Are you for real?" Then, she said yes.

We decided to get married on the premise that we would always be there for each other, and I remembered that she had told me once that, "Nothing you put inside your brain can be taken away."

We talked about our future and our children's future. We figured that with hard work and dedication, we would grow and obtain the things we wanted. We would be able to buy a home, feed and educate our children, take vacations, and keep our faith in God.

It wasn't easy to plan a wedding when I was busy going to school and working, and there were bills to pay. We lived on pennies. Sometimes we had to break the piggy bank just to go grocery shopping. But after months of hard work, we saved enough for the wedding service, our rings, Irene's dress, and the front-store-style hall.

Immediately, we started to plan. We set a date in May, and we decided on a small, affordable ceremony. Though we could not bear the expense of having the luxuries often seen in other weddings, we knew we wanted to be married in a church. So we planned to use Irene's parents' church, First Faith Baptist, and asked family members to each bring a dish for the reception; we would purchase the beverages.

We drove to Canal Street, where many of the jewelry stores in lower Manhattan are located, and shopped around. I had cash and knew I would get the best bargain in one of these stores. Sure enough, she picked one that she liked that was affordable, and I made a deposit on it while she wasn't looking. I returned the following week to pick up the engagement and wedding rings for seven hundred fifty dollars, knowing that I would come back again one day to buy Irene the more expensive ring that we had looked at—the one that I had really wanted to get her.

With plans now in full swing, Irene and I became more confident about our future. We began to relax a little more and have more fun with each other. For example, since I was a hands-on learner, Irene would help me study for my Anatomy and Physiology exam—because she had taken that class in nursing school—while we were in bed. We'd start with the brain and work our way down. And so it happened that, as we made last-minute plans for our wedding, we learned we were expecting our first child.

Thinking about Irene carrying my child, knowing I would soon be a dad, made me put extra effort toward our future. I set goals for myself: to graduate from college before our child turned four and to work toward saving for a house, because I believed in bringing up a family in a home as my father had done. These goals, I knew, were built on the premise that I would get a job working in the lab once I graduated.

We were married as planned, on May 4, 1980. Although the wedding may not have been exactly how we wanted it, we did not put any financial burden on anybody. We had no wedding planner; instead, we did it our way, with our own style. We had no limousine; instead, Irene's father drove us to the reception in his Chrysler (even though it was walking distance from the church). We had no photographer; instead, a friend took snapshots. One of Irene's relatives had a band who entertained us with a couple of songs at the reception. We wrote our own vows, which, without any flowery, formal language, would still last us until death do us part. We did not go on a honeymoon; instead, we had Salaam, were expecting, and were making plans for our future.

Then, just a few months later, in July 1980, Salaam, my pregnant wife, and I joined eighteen of my classmates at a hotel in Manhattan for my graduation ceremony.

My mother, father and sisters celebrate my oldest nephew's birthday

New York Institute of Technology Graduate

Irene on a family vacation

Guys of Victory celebrating Arnaud's 51st birthday

My happy family celebrating the union of Latrice and Patrick.

Chapter 16

Although Irene and I had agreed that I would pursue a bachelor of science degree instead of taking the internship at her hospital's lab, I volunteered to work there anyway, as a phlebotomist technician. I did not mind working without pay, because my mind was set on the future, and I thought the experience would help me find out whether phlebotomy was what I really wanted to do. I worked the six-to-nine morning shift, which was when all of the phlebotomists went up on the floors and took blood from the patients for lab tests.

So every day, after learning how to draw blood, I would go back down to the lab. Through the process, I became acquainted with personnel in the field, and got firsthand observations of the work that would be required of me in such a position. I also came to realize that even with everything I had learned at Mandl, what I knew was minuscule compared to what I'd need to know to work in the field. So I began to ask questions about what I had learned in school, and I learned all they were willing to teach me about being both a phlebotomist and a clerical person at the hospital. I became eager to learn.

Because I was so enthusiastic and showed aptitude, I was allowed to join the elite phlebotomists who did blood work at Schneider Children's Hospital. There, I learned difficult procedures such as how to draw blood with a minimum amount of pain to the young patients. I learned techniques for getting blood from fingers, heels, and veins, and I mastered drawing from premature babies inside the incubator. After my rounds at

Schneider each day, I would then return to do regular rounds with adult patients at Long Island Jewish Medical Center.

After only a few weeks of volunteering, I was officially employed at Long Island Jewish Medical as a phlebotomy technician. Soon after that, upon recommendation of a friend, I applied for an additional phlebotomist position at another hospital, and got it. And so it was that I began working two jobs in two different hospitals.

◆ ◆ ◆

In seeking to further my education, I heard that the New York Institute of Technology offered the program I was interested in, so I took the half-hour drive from our Queens apartment to its Westbury campus. I drove around for a while, found the admissions office, and went inside to get some information. Once I found what I was looking for—confirmation that the school offered a four-year degree in medical technology—I exited the office and got in my car to leave.

Somewhere along the way, however, I made a wrong turn and ended up near the athletic department. I noticed a few guys kicking around on the soccer field, so I decided to stop the car and ask for directions.

As I approached the players, one of them called out, "Hey, Arnaud, what're you doing around here?" I paused to see who it was.

It was Ronnie, a guy I knew from my soccer-playing days with Victory. I greeted him, told him I had been there inquiring about admission, and explained that I was just trying to get back to the main road. He told me how to get out, but then asked, "Are you planning to come to school here?"

"I am thinking about enrolling part time," I told him. "I'm married now, and my wife is expecting our first baby."

We talked for a few minutes, and other players joined in. Ronnie said he was completing his engineering degree and playing goalie for the Bears, after which he told the other guys how good of a player I was. I tried to tell him I didn't play anymore, that my focus was on obtaining a college degree.

As I turned to leave, however, I noticed that, for some reason, my comment seemed only to draw more attention from the team.

"Wait!" Ronnie said, "Don't go yet. I want you to meet someone." Then he suddenly disappeared. I waited. When he came back, he was with a guy in his mid-twenties who looked more like a baseball player, chewing a wad of gum like tobacco. He looked at me, spit on the ground, and with the same breath asked, "Wanna play for the team?"

I was not expecting that. "I don't play anymore," I told him.

"That's not what I just heard from Ronnie," he said. Then he started to talk about getting me scholarship money for tuition and books. I told him that I had not been accepted to the school yet, that I had only been there inquiring. He asked me to follow him to his office, where he told me he was the coach of the men's varsity soccer team. He then called the athletic director, who came in and gave me an envelope. The director told me to take the envelope to the admissions office and they would help me enroll.

I never found out what was in that envelope, but upon receiving it, the secretary in admissions gave me an application. After I filled it out, she took me to the administrator, who asked me if I was ready to take an entrance exam. I looked at my watch. I figured there was enough time before I had to pick up Irene from work this afternoon. Besides, I knew this opportunity was too good to be true.

After reviewing my test, the administrator told me that I would need remedial classes but that it would not be a problem. She then called the athletic department and told the director that I had enrolled.

◆ ◆ ◆

Heading west on the Long Island Expressway back to our apartment in Cambria Heights, I could not wait to tell Irene the good news. She'd known that I'd planned to go to go to NYIT that day after my phlebotomy rounds. But I had only gone to inquire about registering as a non-matriculated student, perhaps taking a class or two while I working as a phlebotomist so that I might, some day, complete my degree. Now, I was headed home with a four-year full-ride scholarship at a private college in one of the most exquisite areas on Long Island.

During the half-hour ride, I thought about the irony of the situation. I remembered all of the rejections I'd received to play professionally and, on the other hand, all of the good jobs I had turned down or left just for soccer. Now, I was about to be twenty-six and a family man, and I had forgotten about soccer at the competitive level. Soccer, however, had not forgotten about me.

At the same time, at my age, and with my now increased responsibilities, I could not help but wonder whether I could handle it all. But because I wanted a degree so badly, I decided I had to be willing to meet the challenge.

As I approached the apartment, all was well. Irene was not to be picked up for another hour, and Salaam's school bus had just dropped him off. He knew right away that I was happy and asked me why. I told him that I was going back to college and that I had a way to pay for it.

I took the frozen meat out of the freezer and a few groceries out of the refrigerator for dinner, then Salaam and I went to pick up Irene. When she heard the news, she was ecstatic. For the rest of the evening, we discussed our new plans for the future. We decided together that while I went to school and played soccer, I would keep the phlebotomy job and also be available on the weekends for extra clerical work at the hospital.

◆ ◆ ◆

On the first day of soccer camp, the entire team had to run two miles in under twelve minutes before we could start our regular practice. I had been up since 5 AM, and had already worked my morning shift at the hospital. That, in combination with the fact that I had not played regularly for years made the run challenging, but I refused to be the last one across the finish line. So I picked out a guy who had the perfect jogging form, and imitated him. I followed him all eight times around the track. When he realized what I was doing, he slowed down for me from time to time, but we still finished among the first group. I had to drag myself to complete the other drills that day, however, and that afternoon, I was sore all over. I was grateful that the nurse in Irene took care of me. She went to the store, bought some Epsom salt, and made me a bath to soothe my muscle cramps.

When I walked into the locker room for practice the next day, the trainer introduced himself as Danny and offered the same treatment Irene had given me. Throughout the remainder of my career at NYIT, I became Danny's regular patient.

The training room was full, with guys getting taped and iced. Afterward, we were all ready to play ball. Instead, we had to run the cross-country trail located behind NYIT. We had two weeks to get in shape before pre-season.

It was not until we played our first scrimmage against another college that I realized why I had been recruited. Although my teammates were all good runners, most of them did not know how to play the game. I had to play hard to cover the younger guys who were playing their first college game.

After that scrimmage, I gained lot of respect from everyone. My experience was apparent, and I received many congratulations. The look in the coach's face showed that he had made the right decision.

◆ ◆ ◆

My first year at NYIT was difficult. Every morning, for three hours before class, I had to draw blood from forty to fifty patients at Long Island Jewish Medical Center. I did the maternity floor and newborn nursery first, which I enjoyed. Everyone was happy. Other floors, however, were not so joyful to work on, at times making my job emotionally stressful.

One day, I was assigned to draw blood from a patient in the psych ward who refused to come out of her room. I was instructed to go into her room to do the job, so I knocked on her door and waited a few seconds before I walked in. The young woman was sitting naked on the edge of her mattress. She had one hand on her vagina, exposing and rubbing it, while she looked at me. At first, I did not know what was going on. I kept looking, expecting her to stop.

Seeming to notice that I was in shock, she then started sucking her lower lip and giving me inviting looks, as she extended her other arm so that I could draw blood. I did not move. After a few moments, I decided to exit the room as calmly as possible. Even if I had chosen to stay and stick her, there was no way I would have gotten accurate blood levels.

I went on to the next patient, where the aide asked me if I had gotten the previous young lady's levels. I calmly asked him to come with me into her room, and when we entered she had on a hospital gown. I drew her blood, but once I finished, she sucked her teeth and asked why I had not done that before. I pretended not to hear her and walked out. As disturbing as the experience was, it changed the way I drew blood from patients on the psych floor; I informed the head nurse of the situation and asked that, from then on, everyone on the floor come out by the nurse's station for blood work.

My rounds also included drawing blood from premature babies to help their physicians monitor them. I would perform heel sticks and sometimes vein punctures. The babies in intensive care were the hardest. Not only were they small, but most of them were also pretty sick. Many times, we lost these babies. The work I did in the neonatal intensive care unit shaped my world, as I realized how sensitive and precious life is.

In addition to the emotional distress caused by patients, I had the normal stress of doing a job that was new to me at the time and very demanding. Every task had to be perfectly done, and I did not want to cause unnecessary mistakes.

Then after work every day, I headed to NYIT, where during my first semester, I took remedial math (because I had not prepared for the entrance exam), biology, and chemistry. After classes, I took a few hours to look at my notes before soccer, and then it was back in the NYIT library until it closed around 10 PM.

NYIT was a great school for me, because it had small classes, which gave me the opportunity to know my professors personally and to get extra help. At any time in my freshman year, I could go to Shure Hall where the Science Department was located, knowing that the professor's door was always open.

◆ ◆ ◆

One morning, I woke up early to hear from Irene that the bed was wet; her water had broken. So we dropped Salaam off at her parents' house and headed to the Long Island Jewish Hospital. We went through admitting and ended up in the labor and delivery room. Our doctor met us there and did an examination, which determined that Irene was ready. Later that morning, however, for the baby's sake, he decided it would be best to perform a C-section. And so it happened that on the morning of October 20, 1980, our daughter Latrice Arnette Bellevue was born.

My boss had let me have the day off, but my coach would not be so kind. I left the hospital with Irene's blessing to play a scheduled game. On the drive there, I felt happy but anxious to get back to the hospital as soon as I could to hold my daughter, and to "play" with her as I had whenever she had moved and kicked inside Irene, and I had rested my head on her belly. I felt that things were finally heading in the right direction, and I was gaining confidence that I would be able to provide for my family as well as or better than my parents had provided for my siblings and me.

At the game, I announced to my team that I had become a father. They just looked at me. No one else was old enough to even imagine what I had experienced that day. A few told stories about younger siblings that their parents had had recently, and then things moved on as usual.

Near the end the game, the score was tied at zero and there was a corner kick toward us. I left my sweeper position in defense and went forward, positioning myself where I thought the ball would end up. Right on the mark, I was blessed with a wonderful goal—the only goal of the night, in fact, and the one that won us the game. Afterward, a reporter from the school newspaper, the *News Day*, interviewed me, and I told him I dedicated the goal to my wife and newly born daughter.

Although I had not done my rounds that morning or gone to any of my classes, I was exhausted. Still, I went straight back to the hospital after my interview, because I wanted to hold my daughter. The problem was, I did not know how. So I received a quick lesson from Irene and the nurse, and then as Irene napped, I lay on the inclined bed next to her and held my newborn daughter. Most of the nursing staff recognized me, so they let me stay in the room a little past visiting hours.

Finally, I left, picked up Salaam from his grandparents' house, and the two of us went home to make room for the new addition. That was when it dawned on me that, soon, this two-bedroom apartment would be too small for us. Fortunately, Salaam was agreeable. He told me that his new sister could share his room and that we would take care of his mom and his sister.

The next day, I took Salaam to the hospital to see his mother and meet his sister. At the time, Irene and I had had several names selected for our daughter that we could not decide upon, so we let Salaam make the final decision.

◆　　◆　　◆

Now that there were four of us, Irene could not work as often as she used to, so I had to make a decision. I either had to quit school and work full time, or find another way to earn more income working part time. I decided to start going to my other phlebotomist job—the one I worked at just sporadically over the weekends—more often, like when soccer was off-season or when I did not have a weekend game. The extra money I earned, little as it may have been, helped us, and in the meantime, I developed a sound work ethic. I worked from early morning to late night, going to school full time, maintaining my athletic scholarship, and working on the weekends without a break. But I was motivated to do so because I felt it was the only way to reach my goals.

Chapter 17

At the end of my freshman year, we were in the post-season play at the finals when my past came back to haunt me. We were playing against Mercy College, and I recognized their coach, not only as someone who had been generally active in the soccer world, but also as one of the coaches from my past who felt I should have played professional ball.

Despite his respect for me as a player, I had to do my best to stay hidden from him. I was afraid that if he saw me, I would lose my athletic scholarship at NYIT. You see, there was a rule in the NCAA that if you have ever tried out for or gone to camp with a professional team, or if you have ever been paid to play the sport, you are ineligible to participate in it again at the college level.

I had heard about the NCAA rule, but did not know whether it applied to my situation. Just in case it did, I had never approached my coach about it, for fear of losing my scholarship. Now, after investing nearly a year of my life into the team and my education, I stood the chance of doing just such a thing.

If I scored, my name would be all over the news, and Mercy's coach would discover it and dig dirt on me. On the other hand, I felt an obligation to score, because the athletic director would be in attendance at this game, looking for a reason to invest more money into our program.

I wanted to beat the other team so badly, but if we scored, it would have to be by someone else. Unfortunately, my teammates depended on me to score. In addition, Mercy was a much better team that year, with a record better than any in its history.

I decided not to panic, to continue to keep the information to myself and to play my regular position in defense. During the game, I set up our center forward many times, but he failed to score. I, too, had opportunities to score, but always passed the ball to other players, who missed the net. Finally, after double overtime, Mercy scored their final goal and won.

Fortunately, however, we also won. Regardless of our loss that day, the athletic director was so impressed with our playing that he gave the soccer program enough additional scholarship money that the coach was able to recruit more players. Many of those recruits ended up being friends I had played with on Victory.

◆ ◆ ◆

When soccer season and my freshman year were over, I took summer classes to clear some prerequisites for the following semester. I also put in more hours at the lab, since classes lasted just a few hours, allowing me to go straight to work afterwards.

In the hematology lab, I answered the phone and entered test results. In the 1980s, the lab at LIJ was not computerized, so we had to enter results manually. It was time-consuming to look up and enter test after test, but I did not mind because it put bread on the table.

My weekend job, which was at a nursing home, provided me with more enlightening experiences. In particular, I saw how fragile life became with age, as, on many occasions, patients would go to meet their maker just when I was about to draw blood.

The first time a patient passed on in my presence, I ran to the nursing station and told the nurse there that the patient had crashed in front of me. I mimicked the way the patient had raised her head and looked at me, before dropping.

"Show me that again," the nurse said. When I did, she laughed and said, "Thanks. We were expecting that to happen—she was a no-code."

I went home and asked Irene what *no-code* meant. She said it referred to a do-not-resuscitate patient. Then I realized the nurse had laughed because of my shocked reaction; although it had been the first time I had seen someone take her last breath, that nurse had probably seen it more times than she had ever wanted.

Turned out, however, that I got used to it too. One morning, it seemed patients were just waiting for me to show up before they died. I had always been nice and pleasant to them, so maybe their spirits were just waiting to see someone they felt comfortable with before leaving. All I know is that on that morning, I saw three of them move on.

After having worked with many sick people, I realized that life was not only about fame, money, and good times. I realized that it was not only about me; now, I had to be responsible for others. So despite my own struggle to improve myself and obtain my degree, I also made sure to enjoy family and friends.

By this time, it was too hard for Irene to work at the intensive care unit full time and take care of Salaam and Latrice, although Salaam was a lot of help with his sister. Adding to the challenge, I was always gone working, taking classes, or playing soccer. We felt Irene's moving her job to the dialysis center in Queens Village would be less stressful for us all. It was closer to the apartment, which, since we shared a car, made it easier for me to drop her off and pick her up from work. And because it offered her working hours that better fit our family's schedule, it allowed us to spend more quality time together.

As parents, Irene and I also tried to shape the future of our family by forming annual traditions. As the kids got older, we gathered for Thanksgiving each year with my brother, his wife Yanick, and their two sons, Hernst Jr. and Vladimir. We would prepare a meal consisting of turkey and Haitian dishes: Griot (fried pork) and Tasso (deep-fried beef), both seasoned with strong flavored pepper; black rice with Haitian spices; black mushrooms; and baby shrimp.

We celebrated Christmas by putting up our tree in front of the living room window, so people could see its lights when they passed our home on Springfield Boulevard.

On New Year's Eve, we would go to First Faith Baptist Church for a potluck dinner. We would have soul dishes like fried chicken, fish, oxtail soup, beef ribs with gravy, collard and mustard greens, boiled cabbage, and black-eyed peas with rice. After eating, we would gather in the church and enter the new year holding hands, praying, and singing gospel music.

New Year's Day dinner would be spent at my mother's house, because it was tradition for Haitians to celebrate the new year with a special pumpkin soup that consisted of either beef or chicken.

Though we may not have realized it at the time, as Irene and I tried to make sense out of life, we were moving upward. And through it all, I became a more mature person, who saw life very differently from before.

Chapter 18

My second year of college was a mirror image of the first, working at two hospitals, playing a varsity sport, and being a father and a husband. I could not slack off in any of these areas, because each one required my utmost. Nonetheless, God provided a way for me to cope with it.

I paid the bills. I gave love to my family. I attended church with them every Sunday morning to worship and to introduce our children to our faith. Practice after practice, game after game, I gave my all to my team. And I managed to compete academically with students who had the luxury of concentrating on their studies and working only part time. As for my social life, I had stopped hanging out with the Victory guys on Friday nights, but it was necessary, and they understood.

In total, my sophomore year was a validation of my commitment toward my goal—not just for me, but for our family.

Something else happened this year, too. It was a small incident, but it made a large impact on me. As there seemed to be increasing incidents in our community that revolved around race, Irene and I began to talk more about current events and reflect on the disparate cultures that she and I came from.

In one such particular conversation, she almost choked when I told her that my experience with racial tension did not begin until I came to America. I explained that in Haiti, the focus had been more on nationality than on race.

Irene, being many generations American, had been taught differently. She openly talked about her country, for whom her father and uncle had fought in the Korean War, but where they could not sit freely on a bus, or eat, drink, or use the bathroom with white people. She felt things were getting better, though, that more people were giving all a fair chance to achieve in America.

I told Irene that I came from a country that had gained its independence from France in 1804, because my dad had been disgusted with the way that independence had been handled. Dad had told Hernst and me that the freedom fighters who had defeated the French had no conclusive plans to lead the country to prosperity. He said the leaders never invested in the country's best interest or future; they wanted to invest in their own interests, regardless of how their financial decisions would hurt Haiti.

Dad's major issue with this all was the government's lack of preparation. There was never a plan to deal with catastrophic issues, jobs, education, and just the general well-being of Haitians. He wondered how a government could allow its country's trees to be cut down without being replaced.

He also told us that Haitian people kept other Haitians from prospering by not giving them the opportunity to do so. For example, after the country gained independence, some Haitians put their own people into slavery, making them work endless hours without any benefits.

My conversation with Irene ended, however, when she said, "I am glad your pops left. If he hadn't, I would have never gotten to know you."

Indeed, she was right.

◆ ◆ ◆

My third year at NYIT came fast. By then, the soccer team had recruited lots of players, and we were making a name in the second-division Long Island league.

By this time, however, I was more focused on academics than on soccer. I was looking into opportunities for my upcoming senior-year internship. In addition, although playing soccer well came naturally to me, I no longer played with a passion, and maybe it was because, physically, I was hurting. I had to play the entire season with a shin splint—chasing around kids just out of high school, no less. At least after my pre-game warm-up, I did not feel pain. But after the game, I had to get immediate treatment just to be able to walk. Spending more time in the whirlpool than usual, I prayed to God that I would not get more injured than I was already, or I might have had to end the season short.

At the end of my third year, the athletic director somehow discovered that I had played soccer for UCCC. He called me, along with his assistant, into his office and questioned me about it. I told him exactly what had happened, and he told me I could not play my senior year. I was off the team. Fortunately, the athletic department saw how hard I was trying in school and was grateful for my contribution to the team, so they agreed to continue my financial support until I completed my degree.

By senior year, I realized it would have been extremely difficult to play anyway. My internship required me to be present at the hospital Monday through Friday from 8 AM to 4 PM. And my wife was expecting another child.

As time-consuming as it all was, however, the internship came as a relief to me. After having worked four years as a phlebotomist, I was prepared to leave the job. I had been waiting for this opportunity for a long time, and Dr. Isenberg had finally helped me get it.

I had crossed paths with Dr. Isenberg many times at LIJ. He was one of the pioneers in the clinical laboratory there, especially in the field of microbiology. Dr. Isenberg's love and dedication to his laboratory was more than admirable to me. Every time I saw him, whether he was right behind me or several yards away, I would hold the door for him and greet him, though I did not know him personally.

One morning, as I was heading upstairs, and he to his office, I introduced myself and told him I was an NYIT student interested in microbiology. Another morning, a few weeks later, I was surprised when he asked me how I was doing in my studies and when I would graduate. This led to continued correspondence between us, which resulted in Dr. Isenberg later signing a letter to the head of the medical technology program that allowed me to do my internship at LIJ instead of the NYIT-affiliated hospital.

Just a few months before getting my degree, on February 13, 1984, we had our second daughter, Cherisse Nikkia Bellevue.

As our family grew, so did my self-assurance. Again, we were bringing a new life into this world, but this time I was more experienced and comfortable caring for her. I now also saw the light of a salary increase, because I knew that soon, I could enter the job market as a college graduate. My job would be union. Irene and I would have a pension for our retirement. Things were looking good.

Then, a few months later, things changed from sweet to bitter, when I heard the most devastating news of my young life.

Chapter 19

Irene, the kids, and I were having dinner when the telephone rang. It was my mother, and she told me that Dad was at Brookdale Hospital in Brooklyn. She did not know what was wrong, except that he had a headache. She said that he'd had a lot of headaches recently, which usually went away when he took something, but that tonight's pain seemed incurable by medicine. Though that didn't sound severe, I was concerned. To my knowledge, my dad had never been to the hospital, and he had always been a skeptic of doing so.

I left my family at the dinner table, got in the car, and sped down Belt Parkway toward Brooklyn. I parked my car and ran into the emergency room, but I did not see him. So I gave one of the receptionists his name. She looked at a chart on the desk and told me he had been there but had since been taken upstairs.

I then asked to speak to the doctor who had taken care of him in the emergency room. I wanted to find out what was going on. They were busy, but finally the doctor came out. He was about my age and of African American or Caribbean decent. He pulled out an x-ray of my father's cranium and showed me an area that indicated a tumor. Although I had no training in radiology, I could tell that the right side of the cranium looked different from the left.

The doctor said that my father had brain cancer, that the type of tumor he had was usually fatal, and at this stage in the cancer, my father had three to six months to live. I asked him whether he had consulted someone in radiology. He nodded. Then he told me that the only way the doctors could even determine whether the tumor was treatable was to perform surgery.

I had to work to catch my breath. It felt like someone had just punched me in the stomach. The doctor must have noticed, because he had been about to go on to the next patient, but then stopped himself. He stayed with me a moment longer, until I had calmed down. I found a chair and sat down, wondering what to do. Then I got up, walked to the pay phone, and called Irene. She said she would be right there.

A few minutes later, the doctor returned and asked me if I was okay. I asked him what he would do if it were his father. He said that he would get the best team of doctors to help him. At the word *help,* I had hope.

I thanked the doctor and then headed to the elevators. As I walked past the entrance, Irene came in. By then, we had purchased a second car, so she had immediately dropped the kids off at her parents' house and driven to the hospital. She and I rode the elevator up and arrived at Dad's room in good spirits. He told us just what my mother had: that he had been having headaches for a while, had been taking medication, and that this time the medication had not helped—the headache had been too much for him. We talked for a while, until his medication made him too drowsy to keep his eyes open. Then Irene and I left for home.

The next morning, we arrived and met with a different set of doctors who were making their rounds. Their prognosis was the same. So we talked to Dad and discussed his options. To our surprise, he said that he'd known for a while that he'd had this condition, because he had been admitted before. But every other time he'd been in, he had been able to sign himself out.

This time was different. My father asked us to find a surgeon who specialized in the kind of operation he needed. Irene and I called around and came up with the name of the head neurosurgeon at New York University Hospital in Manhattan.

We called him, and he agreed to talk to us about my father's case.

When we got there, he and an assistant neurosurgeon examined the films and spoke to their colleagues. Yet again, they gave the same prognosis and the same options, and said that my dad needed surgery as soon as possible. But then, they told us they would not do the surgery, because they did not operate on "everyone." The doctor's inference was that my father was not one of the wealthy patients that the hospital typically admitted for surgery.

I sat in disbelief. Had these doctors just told me that they would not operate on my dad because of a class difference? I wanted to cry, beg, and plead with them, but I just sat there. Apparently noticing the dejection in my face, Irene held my hand and asked the doctors to recommend a surgeon of the same caliber who would perform the operation. After finding out where my dad lived, they recommended the chief of neurosurgery at Downstate Medical Center.

"Do you think this doctor is good enough to operate on my dad?" I asked.

"This doctor has performed enough of this type of intricate surgery that the team there will be able to handle it," was the reply.

Still, as I left their office, I felt very small. Regardless of what happened to my dad, I felt that I just could not give him the best.

My dad showed signs of life, energy, and hope at his examination at Downstate Medical Center, but the neurosurgeon told him that if he decided to have the operation, it should be scheduled no later than next month.

◆ ◆ ◆

The morning of my father's operation, I picked him up from my parents' house in Brooklyn. He told his neighbor, as he got into my car, that he was having an operation and might be back.

I drove him to Downstate Medical Center, which was about ten minutes away. We checked in at the admissions office, and then found his assigned room.

A few minutes later, the nurses and aides arrived and looked around. One of them asked who was having the surgery, and my father flashed them a smile. As the technician and nurses came in and performed their pre-op routine, I stayed and talked with my dad. He told me that they had wanted to operate on him another time, but that he had walked out on them. And he said he was taking a chance with this surgery, that he may not come out alive. He also assured me that if he did die, my mother would be okay.

As we continued to talk, the telephone rang. At first I thought it was my mom, but then the person on the other line seemed to object to his having the operation, because he firmly told whoever it was that he *had* to. As I continued to listen to him talk, it seemed that this other person knew more about his condition than I did.

I sat next to him, praying and hoping that the operation would be successful, and feeling bad that I had not known about his cancer sooner. Then my heart began to race. I walked out into the hallway and cried. The pain I felt was not because someone else had known about his condition before I did and decided not to take care of the problem (although I wasn't happy about that fact, either). I was crying because I had not been there for him. I hurt because I realized I had been so much in my own world that I had not recognized his pain.

When I got back in the room, I know he saw my red, teary eyes. He held the phone up and asked me to talk to his friend, so I did. She asked me whether it was necessary for my dad to have this operation, and I told her that all of the doctors on his case had said the same thing: that he would die if he did not have it. I wanted to ask her how she could have known so much about his condition and not have told him to take care of it, but I did not. Instead, I hung up the phone and just stood there next to my father, as the hospital aides came in and then rolled him away to the operating room.

I left after that to go pick up my mom. We sat in the waiting area for hours, and neither of us had anything to say. Finally, the doctor came out and greeted us. He said that the operation had gone well and that my dad would be coming out to the recovery room where we could see him. I gave my mom a huge hug.

When we walked into the recovery room, my dad was on the bed, raising his head like the elderly patients who I'd drawn blood from so many times. He looked toward my mother and, in his Haitian Creole, said, "It is over. Let's go home." Then his head fell back onto the bed. The nurses and doctors rushed to him and began checking his vital signs.

After a few moments of seeming chaos, the same doctor who had just told us that the operation had been successful was now saying that they had to perform a tracheotomy, and he wanted us to sign a form. We did; however, the second procedure happened too late. Though he was still with us, my father had already said his last words. We would never hear him speak again.

Soon after my dad's second surgery, I walked down to the pathology lab, where I recognized a pathologist who had completed his training at LIJ.

"What are you doing here?" he asked.

I told him about my dad's surgery, and it turned out he was working on that specimen right then.

He gave me a serious look and asked, "Is he conscious?"

"No," I said, "he lost consciousness in front of my mother and me in the recovery room."

The look on his face told me the prognosis was not positive. I asked to take a look at it, but he said it would not be a good idea. "Now, only treatment can determine the future for him," he said, still looking at the specimen and shaking his head.

I went back upstairs and met with the surgeon, and he told me what I had already found out downstairs. The pathology report determined that my father had a grade four glioblastoma multiform, the highest grade glioma tumor, one of the most malignant brain cancers. He said that my father was having a little difficulty now. The doctor could not remove the entire tumor but had removed a tangerine-sized amount. In addition, the surgeons had taken out a significant quantity of my dad's brain.

The doctor's face was not as confident as it had been before the surgery as he told me that my dad was having trouble now, and that all further results rested solely on the radiation. I began to question whether I should have persuaded my dad to have the surgery. I wondered why a surgeon who understood the human body would, even after opening up my dad's head and discovering how much the cancer had spread, still decided to close him and give him the option of radiation, letting him live the rest of his life in misery.

◆ ◆ ◆

The time leading up to my father's death was hard. My dad fought valiantly as I had expected him to. Sometimes, although he could not talk, he would write messages to us on a piece of paper lying nearby, or just make facial gestures or move his legs. Even the slightest movements often gave us hope.

Still, it was difficult for me, because I so badly wanted to tell him that I would finally graduate from college in a few months. Or, more specifically, I wanted to tell him that it was the reason I did not stop by to see him the past six years—because I was working on building my future. The tracheotomy prevented that conversation, however, and his medication kept me from telling him how much I appreciated his leadership and love; as it made him sleep all the time, he wouldn't have heard me anyway.

One time when I went to see him, however, the nurse told me he had been awake all day. Sure enough, as I entered his room, he looked up and saw me. As I approached his bed, he signaled to me that he wanted a piece a paper. I found one and handed it to him with a pen, and wrote, "Am I going to die?"

I did not know how to tell him the pathology report came back with the worst possible diagnosis. I could not tell him that most patients who made it to this room never came out. I could not lie to him about this serious matter, but neither could I utter a word. So I just stood there, tears rolling down my cheeks. He looked at me, took a deep breath, and closed his eyes. I knew my dad knew the answer. The fact that he'd denied treatment for his condition for so long, and only now accepted this surgery, told me he knew this was his only hope—that he knew this was the end of his life.

The radiologist was not optimistic about treatment. He said that most patients at this stage were not affected by radiation. Still, I insisted on it, and Dad did not stop fighting.

Days passed into months. I would walk the halls at different times of the day, and often become panicked to see some body wrapped up on a bed, waiting to be taken to the morgue. I went ballistic one time when I went in his room to find the bed empty. My heart dropped, and I ran to the nursing station to inquire about him, expecting the worst. They told me he was downstairs in treatment.

I went down to his room, but when I got there, what I saw was demoralizing. My dad was on a bed, lying in a fetal position, with a bulge on the right side of his head. The staff was enthusiastic. They were trying to help him.

It didn't take long, however, to conclude that the radiation was not going to work. So they stopped treatment, and I hired a nurse to stay with him during the night. After a few weeks, the nurse called me and said that my dad was brain dead, that she could not take it, and that she would not come back. She never cashed the check I gave her for her service.

After I hung up the phone, Irene and I decided we should go to the hospital to check on him. When we got there, my dad was lying on the bed unconscious and on a respirator. He did not move except for once, when his breathing tube was obstructed by saliva. Irene carefully took the suction device and removed all of the mucus. A nurse walked in and complimented Irene on her technique. The nurse said that she, too, had suctioned him not too long ago, and that a lot of mucus had been coming out of him.

We noticed a lot of stubble on his face, so we asked the nurse to allow us to shave him. She gave us a basin, a razor, and some soap. His eyes were open the entire time Irene and I shaved him.

His condition was deteriorating to the point that it was painful to see him. So that night, I asked God to stop the suffering. Had I stayed a little longer, I would have seen my prayer answered. I had left him a little after midnight, and at six in the morning, we got the call from the neurosurgeon, saying that my father had passed on.

As inevitable as it was, the news was difficult to digest. I could say nothing. The doctor asked me if there was anything he could do and told me that my dad's body was still there if I wanted to see him.

Heartbroken, I thanked the doctor and then called my mom and brother. Then I drove straight to the hospital, but not in time to see my dad. They had already taken him to the morgue.

◆ ◆ ◆

With little experience, we had to bury my father. Fortunately, my older brother's instinct took over, and he contacted the funeral director and made arrangements. My task was to dress him, and we decided that he should be buried in his favorite suit.

I did not want to accept the fact that my dad was dead. And to add insult to injury, some of my father's friends, who probably knew about his condition before I did, claimed that my dad would have never chosen to have the surgery because he knew doctors only operated on people for money. These people knew I was the main person who prompted him to undergo the procedure. Again, I second-guessed myself. Maybe if I had known how long he had been sick, I would have done something different. I had not wanted my father to die without a fight, but had he not gotten the surgery, would he have at least died with dignity?

After being so busy with school for the past six years, this was to have been the year I would enjoy my dad. It was to have been the year that he and Mother would come to my graduation and watch me with pride as I walked down the aisle, just as they had done at my wedding. It was to have been the year that he would have spent with his new granddaughter, and the year I would give him the first paycheck I earned as a medical technologist.

Instead of all that, it ended up being the year we would go to Cypress Cemetery to lay down Dad's remains.

Chapter 20

On an early Saturday morning in June 1984, it finally happened. Irene, pushing Cherisse in her stroller, along with Salaam and Latrice, arrived on the NYIT soccer field, in Old Brookville, Long Island, for my graduation ceremony.

I don't remember much about the ceremony, except for sitting with the graduates, feeling like, now that my dad was gone, a part of me also was missing. Without the support of my wife and the need of our children, I don't think I could have even made it to graduation. The sense of responsibility I felt to model camaraderie and self-discipline for my children is what got me through. It is what helped me focus on the future, regardless of what had happened in my recent past. Unfortunately, although I could see that I was heading in the right direction, there were also bumps in the road ahead, which I could not control; namely, regrets. Regrets that my dad did not live long enough for me to enjoy him, for him to see the progress my siblings and I were making.

My classmates and professors were surprised to see Irene and my three kids. Dr. Spitzer, who had taught my American literature class and frequented our soccer games, introduced himself to Irene and told her how hard he had seen me try. He told her that she deserved half of the credit. Irene's face lit up. He was right. Irene was so proud of me, but she deserved half of my degree. Without her help, without her always having been by my side, graduation would have been impossible.

Dr. Spitzer had been a great help to me over the past few years. We'd first spoken when he had asked me to run a few practices for his son's soccer team. He had noticed some impediment in the way I spoke and offered help. Later, he introduced me to a speech therapist. Now, Dr. Spitzer gave each of us a congratulatory hug, as if in assurance that things would be all right and that our struggle of the last few years would pay off.

Other professors were there too. Dr. Riggins, who taught inorganic chemistry and clinical chemistry; Dr. Muller, who taught biology; Dr. Milocheck, who taught biochemistry, had all given me the support I'd needed over the years to deal with the strenuous science curriculum.

◆ ◆ ◆

Most of the students who graduated with me went on to take the MCAT, which would enable them admittance to medical school; me, I wanted to work.

I gave my resignation letter for the phlebotomist position, when I got an offer to become an on-call medical technologist at St. John's Episcopal Hospital in Far Rockaway Queens. Then during my last few days at LIJ, I was sitting in the hospital cafeteria during my lunch break when the head of the department, Dr. Kanti Rai, came looking for me and offered me a job at his oncology clinic, also at LIJ. The position would be temporary, as I would be filling in for the resident technologist who was out on medical leave, but it would allow me to stay active at the hospital until something else became available, and it was a wonderful opportunity for a job right out of college. In addition, the hours it offered would allow me to keep my soon-to-be job at St. John's.

The oncology clinic provided care to cancer patients diagnosed with either acute or chronic conditions such as leukemia, lymphoma, and multiple myeloma. As a medical technologist, I provided key information to the clinicians to help with the diagnosis and treatment of these patients. During the beginning stages of the illness, the clinician wanted to observe certain components of the blood test. And as the illness progressed, tests would reveal how a patient was reacting toward chemotherapy treatments. I also was responsible for obtaining specimens by doing vein punctures on clinician-ordered lab tests.

So as soon as I graduated, I went on to making a decent income. I was making enough money, in fact, that it did not matter whether Irene worked part time. I worked two shifts almost every day, except Sunday, when I would take the morning off to attend church. Many Sundays, though, I would go to work after church.

As a generalist, I was able to work in all of the labs, as opposed to a lab tech, who specialized in one area. So I immediately started working in different labs and became valuable to the hospital. Often, in front of my small closet-like lab was a line of people, including the head of the department, waiting for results. I really enjoyed that authority as a lab tech.

What I did not enjoy about the job, however, was getting back a bad test result, especially when that result meant that treatment was not working and that the end was approaching. And it was especially painful for me at a time when I was still grieving the passing of my dad.

I saw, from the other side, how devastating cancer could be. On many occasions, I would sit in the lab, where we did blood work on patients after their doctor's appointments next door, waiting for them to gain their composure after receiving devastating news—news like I had heard several months before from my father's neurosurgeon—just so that I could draw blood.

Unfortunately, the doctors couldn't give these terminally ill patients false hope; they had to call it as the x-rays and lab tests showed it. So, because my duties included obtaining blood from these patients, I would try to talk to them and console them prior to vein punctures.

One particular patient in her mid-sixties had been battling chronic leukemia for years, and her doctor had just informed her that the cancer had turned to a more malignant type. She was a wealthy woman, always well-dressed and wearing diamonds, and always chauffer-driven to her doctor's appointments. Since I had begun working with her, she had had an infusaport in her chest area, which is a surgically implanted port that offers entry into a big vein where chemotherapy can be administered and, for some patients, where nursing staff can obtain blood for testing. I sat there, looking at her infusaport, waiting for her to gain her composure so I could do her vein puncture, recalling how I had once perked up my dad after doctors had told him he was about to die. I decided it wouldn't hurt to tell the patient the same thing I had told my dad that day, and it might even help.

"These doctors, they are not God," I said. "Only God will determine when and where you will leave your family. We all will die, and the look in your face doesn't give me any indication that you are about to die." Then I told her not to tell her doctor about our conversation, because most of them didn't know what they were talking about and could die before us anyway.

She stopped crying, pulled out her infusaport, through which her chemotherapy would need to be administered that day, and handed it to me. I told her that I would call a nurse for her, since only nurses were allowed to take blood through the infusaport.

She said that would not be necessary, offered me her arm, and told me that she was confident I could do it. "I'm sure you can find a vein and not hurt me with the needle," she said.

So using the techniques that I had acquired to do vein punctures, I drew all of the tests her doctor had requested, and did so painlessly.

I don't think she told her doctor about our full conversation, but she must have said something to someone because, later, all the doctors and nurses wanted to know what I had said to her. They said that she had changed her attitude so much that her treatments had become effective.

The next time she came, she introduced me to her husband and other members of her family, which made me feel as though she had appreciated my help. This made me feel good, because I felt I had reached my goal of offering her help, giving her hope, and uplifting her, so that she could feel like going on with her life, because she was undoubtedly experiencing her darkest moments. I, too, had experienced such tremendous sorrow, and I wanted both of us to be more cheerful.

◆ ◆ ◆

My family grew yet again on February 11, 1986, when our son Arnaud Jean Roland Bellevue Jr. was born. We included *Roland* in A. J.'s name because it had been the name of his paternal grandpa, whom he had never met.

After A. J., Irene and I decided we were not having any more kids. My coworkers had started teasing me about leaving my wife alone, and, besides, now there were six of us crammed into the small apartment on Springfield Boulevard.

In addition, Irene wanted to go back to work full time, which became possible only because most of our babysitting expenses were absorbed by Mother Wiggins, Irene's mother. I'd often pick up the kids from her day-care center, and instead of paying her, would receive her offer of milk and bread. All of the kids enjoyed her preschool program, which was excellent, complete with nice pictures of their preschool graduation ceremonies.

Mother Wiggins wanted to see us achieve, and because of her, we did. We would not have been able to put money away had it not been for her. She was awesome, and God blessed her with a long life.

◆ ◆ ◆

One gray, chilling Saturday afternoon, I was walking into our apartment when a neighbor called out, "Yo, man! Things getting a little tough? Why don't you go down to the housing office and try to get a three-bedroom apartment? Maybe you can get a subsidized tenement and get a bigger place in the projects."

I paused and looked at him. I did not know how to respond, because we generally didn't talk. But then I realized he was an outsider looking in, and that he was sincere in his effort to help me by telling me something he thought I would not know.

So I took his information, with no intention of using it, and thanked him. I refrained from letting him know that my family was fine and that I had been working for years to obtain a college education so that I wouldn't have to depend on any government agency to give me a free ride. Then, as my ears were beginning to frost over and my toes beginning to freeze, I zipped up my coat, gave him a high five to show my appreciation, and walked into my apartment.

When I got inside, rubbing my hands together to get warm, Irene was standing by our living room window, looking out into the yard. Then she and the kids ran to meet me at the door, wanting to know about the conversation I'd just had with the neighbor.

"We're moving to the projects!" I said sarcastically, and all hell broke loose, especially from Salaam and Latrice, who were old enough to understand what I'd said but too young to understand that it was a joke.

Latrice looked at me and said, "Dad blew it!"

Salaam, probably recognizing the smile on my face, grabbed Latrice's hand and pulled her to the sofa. "We're not moving to the projects," he assured her.

"Un-hun," Latrice replied, "Daddy said we are moving there."

Salaam explained to her that that would never happen to us, because Dad had been to school and had a good job.

As Irene left to continue her chores, I sat down on the couch next to them. Latrice jumped up on my leg and gave me a big smile to let me know she got my joke. She was missing her two front teeth, which reminded me of the phone call I'd gotten just a few days before. Grandpa Wiggins had been on the line. He had been very concerned as he told me about how Latrice had fallen while playing at the day care and knocked her teeth out. He sounded worried that I would be upset and was warning me before Irene came home with her, so I calmed him down and assured him that I thought it was okay.

When Latrice got home, she ran up the stairs, teeth in hand, and looked at me. "My teeth came off," she said, opening her little fingers to show me. "Fix it."

"How?" I smiled at her.

"Put them back," she said, pulling back her upper lip to show me the space.

I cuddled her and looked to make sure that the teeth had broken cleanly, that there was no tooth left in her gum. I told her that since they were her primary set of teeth she was lucky because they would grow back. She asked if they would grow before tomorrow when she returned to school.

Now, as Irene washed the clothes, cooked dinner, and warmed A. J.'s milk, I sat cuddling her again, sitting on the couch, thinking how, though our apartment was tight, it was full of love. In fact, I had begun to enjoy our home for its closeness. If someone needed to sit down next to any one of us on the couch, without even uttering a word, we would make room. We would push the dining room table against the wall to make space to get to the kitchen, and then pull it out again so we could sit together for home-cooked dinners. Then Salaam and Latrice would do their homework at that table, as Irene and I either watched, cooked, or washed clothes. The one thing I could not get accustomed to, however, was going to the laundromat to dry our laundry, because there was no room for a dryer in our apartment.

Still, after this six or so years, I had grown more confident than ever that this would not be our permanent home. Confident enough that I finally told Irene we had to look for a house. She looked at me like I was crazy. She knew we did not have enough money for a down payment and closing fees.

With what little we had in the bank, we hired a real estate agent to find out what was required to buy a home. Other than a couple of six-month certificates of deposit worth about twenty-five hundred dollars, the only commodity we had was the fact that we both had professions and were college graduates.

We learned that if we put twenty percent down, we would not have to pay for mortgage insurance. Since we told the real estate agent that we had four kids, were not expecting any money from relatives, and would be living on our own, she suggested we put ten percent down and pay for the insurance until the equity in the house exceeded twenty. I wrote down everything she told us. Irene was discouraged. She was sure we would not be able to save the required twenty to twenty-five thousand dollars. I was not worried.

As we spent time looking at different houses in the Queens and Nassau County areas, we made do with the Mustang Mach 1 hatchback gas-guzzler we had purchased from a member of our church as a second car. Our income had grown to exceed our expenses, the biggest of which were rent, Salaam's private school, and Latrice's Montessori school. During non-school hours, Mrs. Williams, one of the church members, babysat all of the kids for us for next to nothing. On Fridays after we paid her, she would bake us a sweet potato pie.

We had help from everyone. From Mother Wiggins to Sister Williams to Reverend Wiggins to all the members, siblings, and friends of First Faith Baptist Church, everyone always commended Irene and me on how we had struggled thus far with the children. But without their help, I would not have been able to work the countless hours of overtime that I did, which is what helped us to save our money so quickly.

When the resident technologist returned from medical leave, LIJ asked me to remain on staff at the oncology clinic for at least two to three shifts a week, and I continued to go to St John's Episcopal as my schedule allowed. In fact, oncology was planning to give me full-time employment by then, because they needed an extra technologist. At the very same time, another opportunity presented itself in the microbiology department where I had done my internship. The human resources department told me I was hired before I even filled out the application. So this became my third and main job, which I worked 4:00 PM to midnight Monday through Friday.

I celebrated with Irene, who always said I would be working in microbiology. Over our usual sparkling champagne, as the grin on her face and the sincerity in her eyes made me believe she knew I would be successful, we decided to buy the solid brick house we had liked. It was four-bedroom, finished-basement house in a nice, quiet community in Queens Cambria Heights.

We had decided that we wanted to stay in Cambria Heights. We were accustomed to the area, and it was where we wanted to raised our children. We'd just wanted more room and to be away from the main boulevard. We'd also wanted to be in a quieter, safer, more family-friendly part of Cambria. As an added bonus, here, we would not have to pay the inflated prices of houses we'd seen in other areas.

I had to do some creative financing to find the down payment and closing costs. Because we anticipated a solid future income in addition to what we had saved, and because we had a decent credit rating due to our paying our bills on time, we were able to borrow additional money at a very high interest rate. When we were approved, I envisioned how Dad, every payday, would sit on the edge of his bed writing checks to different creditors. When one of us walked in the room, Mom would be lying next to him, and Pop would lecture us on the importance of paying bills on time.

And so it happened that we moved into our first house in July 1986. It was an exciting experience for all of us. We now had plenty of space, and it was a big difference for the children, who no longer had to ask if they could go outside to play.

The house had a front and a side entrance. The long driveway led to a garage and a backyard, where the kids played and Irene and I barbequed. The side door would open and slam shut as the kids freely enjoyed going out into the hot, sunny days of summer.

Our timing in the market was great, too; we had not anticipated the value of homes to increase further, because the real estate market had just experienced a boom.

There was work to be done, however. We did landscaping and installed a fence. We also had more chores to do than were necessary in the apartment. We had anticipated all of the additional tasks, but now, we had to live it.

Ultimately, I felt that I finally had a profession that enabled my family to depend on me. Before, the jobs I'd had—even those at Dunn and Bradstreet and at Phillip Brothers—had been lies. I had not put in the time and schooling that I had claimed to put in for those early jobs. Now, I experienced a sense that I was trustworthy. I was working honestly in a profession that would allow me to be a provider for my family.

Chapter 21

One morning at work, I was on break but not in the mood for conversation, so I retreated to the corner of the break room, where Charlie always sat. Charlie worked in the research lab. He was about my height and in his early- to mid-thirties. His eyes always looked strained and red, like he'd been up all night long, and at break time, he always sat in the corner reading the *New York Times* science section.

Today, I looked down at one of the sections he'd put on the table in front of him and an article caught my curiosity. I asked him if I could borrow the paper, and he nodded and continued to read. After finishing, I discussed the article with him, which led to a more in-depth conversation about why he always occupied that corner of the cafeteria and was always reading.

"I'm about to finish this program at Columbia," he said.

"Which program?" I asked.

"It prepares you to take the MCAT. It only requires that you have a BS degree in science."

"Yeah," I said, "but—"

"No *but*, man. It only takes a few semesters of classes after work, and if you have a B-average, Columbia University will vouch for you when you apply to medical school." Then he told me about another employee who used to work at LIJ. "He completed the program and is now in his second year at medical school."

"Unbelievable," I told him.

"I'm almost done," he said. "After this physics class, I'll sit for the MCAT."

"Good luck," I said, as our break ended and we headed our separate ways.

That conversation stuck. What he'd said made sense to me: if I had gotten this far, why not continue? Charlie was doing it, and he had a family like I did. So the next time I saw him, we exchanged numbers. He called me a few weeks later, right after he took the MCAT, and reiterated that there would have no way he could have succeeded had it not been for the program. He gave me a name and number for the person to talk to at Columbia University. Soon after, he went on to medical school.

As with all of my previous ideas of this magnitude, I laid the idea out for Irene, but this time knowing that the walls of the room in which we sat had expanded, along with our bills and responsibilities. Fortunately, she was very happy about the idea, because by this time, I had convinced her that I achieve whatever I put my mind to. She also liked the idea that her husband could become a doctor. So Irene decided she would resume a full-time job as a nurse, and for the moment, we forgot about our four children and the fact that we had just purchased a home.

The next day, I called the number Charlie had given me and made arrangements to speak with a counselor. The counselor was very professional. He explained the program, and he remembered Charlie. I registered for one class as a non-matriculated graduate student, and to get my feet wet, took just the first of the four to five required classes that the counselor had recommended. He stated that those courses, along with the undergraduate program I had already done, would be enough for me to sit for the MCAT.

As I sat in the lecture hall in my first class, cellular biology, I observed the students around me, who likely had just finished their undergraduate degrees and now sat comfortably to become neurosurgeons, cardiologists, and other cream-of-the-crop specialists. These students seemed so different from those in the many other classes I had attended throughout college. I felt I did not belong. But I had been given a chance, so I had to take it.

Class after class, the materials required time and effort. As in all science classes I had taken, as the semester progressed, the class became smaller. When it came time for the midterm, I did not do as well as I wanted.

As class let out, I stayed seated for a while to clear my mind. Many groups of students passed me by, and their level of concentration and dedication was clear. Being a doctor was definitely for those who were not only willing to sacrifice and put their minds to the task, but those who were able. If I were to be successful, I would have to alienate my kids and Irene and destroy what meant much more than living an unattainable dream.

I left class and walked down Broadway, toward One Hundred Twenty-fifth Street. There, less than a mile away, the atmosphere was very different. Even though it was the middle of the day, businesses had no vigorous customer traffic, as did the ones by Columbia. People seemed to be just walking around to pass the time, as if they had no destination, either in town or in life. This new culture took me by surprise. Even though I had not expected an Ivy league atmosphere, I'd thought that at least there would be some sense of hope for the future in the faces of these people who passed me by.

I circled and returned to the train station from which I had taken the E-Train for nearly two years while attending Mandl. By the end of the night, I had wandered in Upper Manhattan to Harlem, and had watched people. I had seen in everyone, regardless of race or gender, looks of belonging, striving, and wanting to change their lives. There was no doubt that the future of these two worlds were so close to each other and yet so far. Upon further examination, I found myself in the middle, in our house with four wonderful children and enjoying the fruits of our labor.

I had a decision to make. I realized that here before me was a perfect opportunity. However, taking advantage of it would mean taking time off to study. And there were the kids and other responsibilities that came with being a husband and a dad. I could not ignore such responsibilities.

The rest of that semester, I continued to attend classes, because the lectures fascinated me, but I did not continue to medical school. If I had given up what Irene and I had created, I would never have been happy again.

The next day, as we sat in our living room, deciding on new furniture, I looked around at my family, and found all of the reasons to be happy and content. And I realized that up until now, although I had been working at improving myself, I had still felt lost and confused.

"What are you thinking about?" Irene said. I looked up at her. "Let's go." I looked at the clock and realized we had to leave for her dentist's appointment. On the way there, Irene said, "Honey, how would you feel if I asked the dentist how much it would cost to close my gap?"

"Uh, what?" I responded. "Close your gap?"

"Yeah! I always wanted to close my gap. Everyone has always teased me about my gap, and now we both have insurance."

"Honey," I said, "you without your gap, to me, would be like missing one of the four seasons."

We both laughed. But after subsequent visits, Irene's gap disappeared.

Chapter 22

Salaam had begun making music on his computer. He explained to me how the computer worked, how the sounds were independent of one another until he synchronized them to make music. He told me this was the new way of making music and he was really into it.

Salaam was so interested in making his music on his computer, and I wanted him to concentrate on his studies. He was getting older, and he felt that he could no longer hide his music from me. I would go into his room and have him stop playing it, and no sooner had I exited the house, his room was in the front by the driveway where I parked my car, I would hear the music again. I told him that music would land him nowhere, but a life that would be insecure and unreliable. I told him that he needed to pursue his studies and his life would be better in the future. I told him of musicians who had not made it and how the disappointments had affected their lives and those few who were successful faced other problems.

Salaam, who had never disrespected me nor showed disagreement, told me that his style of music was different. He tried to educate me about this new form of music. He called it "remix." He gave me a lesson on how he had coordinated remix music. Although it sounded good, he did not make a believer out of me. So I went downstairs and spoke to Irene. She was neutral. I thought that Salaam needed to be studying because he was in high school. He needed to prepare himself to be a college graduate and to excel higher than me and Irene. I was talking to him about becoming one of the students at Columbia and becoming a doctor, lawyer, or other professional with a stable income.

Irene told me she understood my concern and, surprisingly, told me to allow him to follow his dreams. Irene said maybe that was Salaam's calling.

All of this did not impress me the way he wanted it to. I saw the disappointment in his face as I told him my opinion about people who unsuccessfully make music. As a concerned parent, I told him that he should concentrate on his school work instead. Salaam was not a disobedient child and so acquiesced as he had always done. But until now, I had not noticed that Salaam often disagreed with my opinions.

Salaam had always ridden with me to and then watched me at my soccer games and practices. At home, I made him run around and kick the soccer ball. I would take him to the local Haitian barber who would give us haircuts; by the look on Salaam's face, I could tell he often didn't like his haircut, but he'd never complained about it. He simply did these things because I asked him to. And now, after all we had been through together, we were about to disagree on something that meant a lot to both of us. Fortunately, Irene handled the conflict between Salaam and me with grace. She made me realize that Salaam was young and that we should let him follow his dreams. She said we should share the love and admiration that Salaam had for his music and that this was how he would develop his passion further.

Irene had allowed Salaam to have his music-making computer in the first place because she also loved music. She was raised in a family who loved and sang gospel music. As a youngster in Harlem, she had also sung in the family's church choir, and did so to this day. She had let him have the computer after we'd moved to the house, because Salaam had had to give up his full set of drums that he played at the apartment; the neighbor downstairs kept knocking on the door, screaming that she was trying to get some sleep, and then his sister and, later, his other siblings were born. In the house, however, he was more comfortable. He had more space to venture and create his beats. When I was not home, he would also serenade his mother and his brother and sisters and anyone who happened to pass by his window. So it seemed I was the minority in the house who could not comprehend his love for his music.

The house, especially the backyard, had also given Latrice, Cherisse, and A. J. the freedom to grow up and carry out their mischievous acts. They played up and down the stairs, inside and outside. So it wasn't a mystery when Irene started getting fatigued. We both figured that she was working too much and that as the kids were aging, they were becoming too much for her to handle along with work. So we agreed she should slow down and work only a few days a week; and later, when the kids were older, she would resume working full time.

We hired people to help Irene with the kids, but that did not go too well because Irene had her ways. She was a strong-minded person, and after a few weeks of rest, she felt better and wanted to continue full time, and even work overtime, because we were now dreaming of buying another house and maybe even another after that.

After buying our first house, she had become really ambitious, because we saw the enormous amount of wealth that people had, and it now seemed reachable to us as well.

◆ ◆ ◆

In a telephone conversation with my brother Hernst, we decided to investigate how to make money by owning a business. In particular, we wanted to research how we could open a franchise. And it was such that my brother, who had an MBA from Long Island University in Brooklyn where he studied finance, and I decided to invest in a Subway sandwich franchise.

As Irene and I discussed our part of the investment in this venture, she fell asleep, but her love and admiration were evident, as was her support for the idea. So Hernst and I drafted the preliminary application. Not much later, he received a call stating that we had been approved by the Subway franchise as a potential franchisee but that we had to meet certain conditions before we could open a store; namely, we had to undergo training. To do so, we would have to go to Connecticut for two weeks.

So Hernst and I took vacation time from our jobs, and each day, drove the two-hour commute, usually in the snow, to Connecticut and back—four hours total. We joined franchisees from all over the United States to learn how to open and operate stores.

We had the choice of staying in a hotel as everyone else did, but we decided that by commuting, we would save the money we'd need later for opening the store. Because we traveled every day, we missed a couple of the evening events (franchisees could not believe we didn't attend the party at the Subway founder's house), but it was our choice. Besides, we liked to use the long commutes to study our test materials. When Hernst was driving, I would read out loud and then we would discuss the topics. He would do the same when I drove.

We knew it would be a challenge, but we were determined. And after completing the course, passing all of the finals, and taking an internship, our determination paid off: in 1988, my brother and I were certified at the Subway headquarters in Connecticut, and granted our license to operate a Subway franchise.

After completing franchise school, with the help of a Subway representative, we looked at areas where we might want to open a store. All of the areas I liked presented a problem for the representative. Some were too expensive; others had crime rates that were too high. We ended up at a strip mall in North Hempstead near Garden City, in a store formerly occupied by Allstate insurance.

Now we had the task of turning the building into a franchise complying with Subway. So after signing a ten-year lease, it was time to begin construction. Although we were guided, the major decisions were ours. We decided how we would situate the store, how much area would be designated for our office space, where the soda machine would be located, and even how customers would enter and exit the store.

We had so many decisions to make, and the process was complicated by the fact that we both had to juggle our time between work and the construction site. We discussed in our pre-opening plans that I would work the morning shift, stopped going to the oncology lab, and reduced my hours at St. John's Episcopal, while Hernst would close the store and keep his morning job. For the few hours that lapsed, we would depend on hired help. And for me, things just kept getting more difficult, because Irene kept getting more tired.

Her fatigue never slowed her down, however, even when it came to just hanging out with me and the kids. We'd gone to concerts, Broadway shows, and church gatherings. But after these events, she'd be so exhausted and out of it that she'd sleep in the car on the way home.

Then one afternoon, Irene and I were on the bed napping, when our alarm went off. I had to go to work, and Irene had an appointment to do home dialysis on one of her patients. Irene said that she could not move and asked me to help her up, because she wanted to go to the bathroom. I ignored her request, thinking she was joking. I thought she wanted to play, because we both had been working so hard with the children, the house, and our jobs. I told her she should stop it and get up to go do what she had to do.

When I didn't get a response, I opened my eyes to see if she had gotten my message, and rubbed my hands on her shoulders to encourage her to get up. Then, Irene told me she felt much better and not to worry about helping her to the bathroom. By saying that, she got my attention. She hadn't been kidding at all.

So I looked at her, and saw that one side of her face looked as thought it were paralyzed. And as she got up to walk to the bathroom, I saw she had a somewhat different gait. She was struggling; one side was pulling the other as if it had a ten-pound weight attached to it. When she came back out of the bathroom, she was pulling herself the same way. One whole side of her still look as if it was paralyzed.

I immediately called work and told them I couldn't come in. Then I called Irene's patient and told her that Irene would not be there, and I had Irene call someone to cover her patient. Finally, I called a neurologist I had met at LIJ and explained that my wife appeared to be experiencing neurological symptoms. I told him what had just happened to her, and he asked me about her current condition. So I asked Irene how she was, and she told me she felt fine. I looked up at her face to see that it seemed to have returned to normal. She also seemed to be walking normally again. The doctor told me that if we noticed the symptoms again, we were to immediately go to the ER.

That night, I could only hope that I was being an overprotective husband, that the incident was just a fluke. And looking at Irene right then, who appeared as if nothing had ever happened, gave me a false sense that everything would be all right.

As days went by and things returned to normal, we followed our regular routines and missed her scheduled appointment with the neurologist. However, after a while, I noticed a slight deficiency in Irene's walk. She favored one side. And she continued to experience weakness and fatigue. So I called the neurologist again, and this time, he told us to come straight to his office.

After the examination, the doctor asked Irene to stay outside in the waiting room. He then took me to his office and told me that Irene's neurological condition resembled multiple sclerosis. My heart sank. The doctor told me that he was not positive Irene had MS but that if she did, he could not help; we would need to find a highly specialized neurologist. He also said that if Irene had MS, her condition would get indefinitely worse.

I began to question the doctor's skill. I wanted to drop to the floor. But then, somehow, I immediately felt a tremendous uplift in my spirit, a sense of determination that whatever happened, I would deal with it. I would do whatever it took to fight and win. I had no doubt that there was something medicine did not know and had not experienced about this disease, and I was determined to find it and help Irene.

It presented a challenge to tell Irene because, as a registered nurse, she knew too well about this debilitating disease. But it was a necessary evil. So Irene came back into the office and sat down. The neurologist quickly broke the news to her, and there was a pause. I looked at her, knowing that she was devastated but that she would not let the doctor see how it had affected her.

We left the doctor's office speechless. The twenty-minute ride home felt like an hour.

Over the next several days, we started to put the pieces of the last few months together. Irene had needed to get an eye examination to have her eyeglass prescription adjusted (MS affects a person's vision). We also found out that the incident in the bedroom, when Irene had not been able to make it to the bathroom, was typical of an exacerbation from this disease. When we did, she realized that she had had several mini-exacerbations before that one. We had just attributed them to her being tired and stressed, from our moving to a bigger place, having four increasingly demanding children, and her working full time as a nurse.

Now, all of the dreams that we'd had were no longer important. Before, we had wanted to accumulate financially. We had wanted to invest in our children's education, buy real estate, and take vacations. The news of possible MS tempered those goals, as we became more focused on my wife's health.

That weekend, Irene exacerbated again. We went to the ER at LIJ, and the neurologists confirmed the diagnosis. They performed several blood tests and also did a spinal fluid examination. Upon hearing this, Irene looked at me and told me that, from her experience as a registered nurse, the diagnosis was on-point. I held her hand and told myself with all my heart and strength that we would fight this. She was admitted for observation, but as with her other episode, she improved quickly.

Days after that exacerbation, however, she became progressively weaker, so we inquired about other hospitals that specialized in MS. Irene's cousin, a physician, recommended Columbia Presbyterian Hospital in Upper Manhattan.

By the time we saw the neurologist there, Irene's gait had become apparent to the trained eye. As was the entire staff at Columbia Presbyterian, the neurologist was very knowledgeable. She reaffirmed the diagnosis, adding that Irene would probably never get better. She said that the only way to treat MS in America at the time was to administer steroids. And she told us that to receive such a treatment, Irene would have to be hospitalized and tested, after which she could receive the medication intravenously. At least we had hope—the hope that this steroid would work.

We drove in silence to Irene's parents' house, where we had to pick up the kids. When we walked in, we noticed Cherisse holding her nose. When we asked what was wrong, she showed us the cut she had gotten while playing outside. Irene looked at it, washed the area with peroxide, and determined that we would not have to take Cherisse to the emergency room. As she cared for her daughter, Irene's gait was not as noticeable. Still, we took the extra time we had at her parents' house to break the news to them.

Not understanding MS, her parents just seemed happy that we were seeking treatment, which, along with their faith in God, they hoped would ultimately remedy her condition.

◆ ◆ ◆

Every piece of literature I researched, every doctor I spoke to, every medical journal I read all had the same prognosis: multiple sclerosis is a fatal disease and our only alternative was steroid treatments. Other than that, medical professionals did not have an answer to our dilemma. The intricacy of it was beyond even the best-educated medical professionals, who could only observe and document how different patients dealt with the horrible disease. (To give you an idea of the depth of common knowledge about MS at the time, we were told by many that it was an old Jewish people's disease.)

But Irene and I determined that we had come a long way; we had had four kids together and, so far, had accomplished all of our dreams and goals. We were not going to give up now.

We had a wonderful family because of the hard work and dedication of Irene. She was the nucleus of our family, my friend, and my sponge. Now, all that I had read were indications that she would die a cripple. I was pretty defiant about accepting that. The greatest medical professionals were telling us there was nothing that they could do but inject her with steroids. I was livid; I was not prepared for that kind of news. Although I had experienced my father and mother both having surgical procedures, they had a chance. The doctors could not surgically remove the nerve ending that was believed to affect patients with MS.

So Irene and I made arrangements for treatment at Dr. Britton's clinic at Columbia Presbyterian. Before administering treatment, the doctors had to rule out diseases that mimic MS, so they tested for Lupus, Lyme disease, AIDS, and other conditions.

During Irene's first visit with Dr. Britton and the other neurologists, Irene told them about the episode that had occurred when she had her first major exacerbation, which was immediately after she had had her dental procedure. She told them, "Immediately after that root canal I did not feel normal. I felt it was probably a reaction from the anesthetic that the dentist had used." The doctors told us that it was a coincidence and that they were not related.

After the tests, the doctor took me aside and gave me the formal diagnosis: that Irene had progressive degenerative multiple sclerosis, that patients with that form of MS do not last more than two years, and that treatment would not be a cure but only a way to prolong her life.

I sat there. I could not get up from my chair. So the doctor got up from hers and came over and rubbed my shoulder. It caught my attention because, in my experience, doctors had seldom showed sympathy. I was finally able to get up and go deliver the news—to my wife, my kids, our family, and our friends.

I returned to Irene's room, and she wanted to hear what I had to tell her. Once I did, she sat there. But we decided that she was not going to die. I told her that she would live to see her four children grow up. She wanted to go on with the treatment.

The doctors at Columbia Presbyterian carefully monitored her and gave her major doses of Prednisone and treated her for all of the side effects of this medication.

After the first treatment, she had to stay at the hospital to receive therapy for weakness in her left leg, which she had incurred from her most recent exacerbation. And it was after this point that I noticed a sudden change in her personality. Because of the steroids, at night she thought she was a nurse working on the floors. She would help other patients until one patient's family complained to Dr. Britton.

But after a little more than a month, Irene came home a mega woman. She had responded very well to the treatment, and was back on her feet, running the house. She returned to work at LIJ with a cane to help her balance her slightly deficient gait. I thought that was the end because she looked good and energetic.

Meanwhile, in early summer, Hernst and I opened our Subway store. But by this point, I no longer had the same goals. Making a lot of money was not my priority.

Regardless, I put in my time because I had already committed myself to and spent a lot of time with my brother. Because we always wanted one of us to be at the store, we alternated shifts. I was responsible for the morning shift, and my brother came in for the evenings.

Fortunately, Salaam was a great help, just as he had always been—even back at the apartment when he would take care of his two sisters. Now he gave us his precious teenage time to help us with his brother. We were very grateful that he had such a caring attitude, not to mention so much love for his family.

Chapter 23

Hopeful that the MS would not be as devastating as other cases we read and heard about, we shared the diagnosis with only close family and friends. We kept up with our daily routine as if everything were normal.

My biggest fear, besides Irene's health and well-being, was how we would cope with the change in her health status, and how that would affect the kids, who were still relatively young.

Our plans for the kids continued with only a few adjustments; we decided they would go to the public school in Cambria Heights until sixth grade, and after that we would provide them with private education.

I took it one day at a time, and Hernst and I continued with the store as I juggled my time between two hospitals. I was concerned about our future. Irene and I had planned that, after we opened the Subway store, eventually I would stop working at least one job to help Hernst grow a chain. Meanwhile, she would work full time to maintain some kind of steady income. Now, I began to question this decision. I knew that Irene going back to work full time was not an option, but that sharing the profit from only one store with my brother would not be enough to maintain our standard of living. At the same time, I felt obligated to make it work, because my brother and I had made such a large investment of time and money into the store.

Then reality set in. The late hours and the demanding work required of us to maintain the store were overwhelming. And I did not want to be away from home so often now that Irene's health was deteriorating. Deciding that the sandwich business was not worth leaving our jobs, we hired a manager, instead, as well as other staff. Then eventually we sold the store to this guy who claimed bankruptcy soon after, resulting in lost money.

Meanwhile our kids were growing up and incurring different needs, and our family dynamic was again changing. Soon after Salaam graduated from high school, he moved out to start his music career. Latrice, Cherisse, and A. J. were also getting bigger. We bought a new Lincoln Continental and a time share in the Poconos, where we spent family vacations and I learned to play golf.

Irene's MS went into remission, and we were hopeful it would go away. We hoped it would be the type that would allow her to enjoy her young and growing family for many years to come. She would drive the kids to many of their school events. She'd go to A. J.'s kindergarten class to help serve at parties, and on overnight field trips with Latrice's school. She would also make several trips to the hospital to care for her ill father.

Then one day, while driving, with the kids in the car, she experienced blindness. Latrice had to tell Irene at the full stops whether other cars were coming. Luckily, she was near the house, and they made it home safely. Unluckily, the same weekend, she lost her ability to walk.

◆ ◆ ◆

"Nothing … nothing," our ophthalmologist, Dr. Fox said as he examined Irene's eyes. Then he looked at me in disbelief and repeated it again. "Nothing. There is no activity in Irene's eyes at all."

As she wept for about the tenth time about how her body had hopelessly deteriorated, Irene asked, "Is there a surgery that can be done to restore my eyesight?"

It was the most difficult time in my thirty-five years on this earth. After we had worked hard to get married, educate ourselves, and become providers, we now faced having a life tainted by disability. My wife, a woman who had always been independent, caring, and loving, had become totally dependent on the care of others.

Though we were going through the pain, we absorbed it. We did not want anyone to share it with us, especially the kids. There were always signs from above that would show me the way and get me through the day.

When Latrice was in fifth grade, her class went on an overnight field trip to Boston. Irene was still walking with a cane and, though it was still months before she'd lose her eyesight, she was already sporting thick eyeglasses. In addition, I had sustained an injury to my Achilles tendon, so was also was limping as we boarded the bus that mild, sunny morning. Though Irene was not going on the trip, she had been able to drive us to the spot from where the three buses full of fourth and fifth graders were to leave.

Latrice got on the bus and proudly announced me. Truly, I felt a bit uncomfortable, but I had already promised Latrice that I would chaperone. Among the many other parents and teachers waving and wishing us a pleasant voyage, Irene stood leaning on the front driver's side door of our burgundy Lincoln Continental, waving us good-bye. The kids were so excited. I, however, was a bit nervous. It was my first overnight trip because, had Irene been able to go, I would not have stood a chance.

After dragging myself around all day, following the itinerary—which included visiting places involving the American Revolution and one of the first Anglo-Saxon churches—I found myself at the end of the line of kids. We concluded the day by checking into our hotel, after which we ended up in the swimming pool and I ended up in the right place at the right time.

This young lady was drowning in front of me, and there was no way for anyone but me to notice; the lifeguard had his hands full, because there were so many kids in the pool. I saw a head going down, and it was apparent it was a girl because I saw long braids, with two ribbons attached to each. Carefully, I pulled on her arm and let it go. When it dropped, I realized what was happening. I quickly pulled her up and swam with her to the side of the pool, where I realized that, because of my injury, I could not jump out of the pool. I yelled as loud as I could to the lifeguard, who rushed over and started to give the girl CPR.

As he did, something at the bottom of the pool caught my eye. I saw what appeared to be a small object. I dove in to see what it was, and as I approached it, I noticed that it was a polka-dotted swimsuit on another young girl, who was in a limp, rag-doll position. I grabbed her and pulled her through the water, ending up at the other side of the pool. This time, I forgot about my Achilles tendon because this young girl's face was blue.

As the lifeguard approached us, he had a confident look on his face. His light green eyes looked at me, stunned, but with a confidence that said he knew what to do. Swiftly, he secured the girl's head, and with two fingers, he pressed her nose shut as he had done with the other young lady who was now okay—but this time, nothing. He looked at me with desperation, and I took over. There was not any pulse, but we managed to massage her and get a pulse back. And that's all I remember. After the incident, Latrice told me that, as I had been giving the girl CPR, I had been begging, "Please, please, please give me a pulse."

After being admitted to the hospital for observation, both young ladies came out okay.

Chapter 24

One of the blows that MS dealt was that, though Irene's physical body was deteriorating, her mental functions remained perfect. And because she had always been a woman who was fashionable and wanted to look her best, I would now spend hours getting her ready. I would help her out of bed, to the bathroom, and then helping her prepare herself so that no one would see her weakness. Though she was confined to a wheelchair and had lost her eyesight, she felt that she would get better. She did not want to give up. I looked at her, and she gave me inspiration and strength.

In addition, after her second hospitalization with intravenous Prednisone, Irene gained a lot of weight. To lose it, even though she was blind and disabled, she managed to get an appointment with Dr. Atkins at his Manhattan office without my help.

You see, after Irene had lost her eyesight, I did not know what to do. Then, one night, an idea came to me. After completing my shift in the microbiology lab, I sat next to her on our king-sized bed. I moved closer to her and reaffirmed how beautiful she was and how much I loved her, and I told her that nothing would ever separate us. She said that from now on, she would take the diagnosis of MS to mean "More Strength." Then, as I held her in my arms, I told her that I had an idea to help her use the phone and eat independently. She listened to me as I held her hands and showed her the keys on our telephone. She used our technique until one of the telephone providers offered a voice-activation service. After that, she regained her connection with people, and that allowed her to make the appointment with Dr. Atkins.

To get her into our Lincoln, I would hold her at the waist and bend my knees to lift her, so I wouldn't hurt my back. As I lifted her, she would always remind me. "Are you bending your knees? We can't have both of us disabled." So I would bend even more. Then when I got her situated in the passenger seat, I folded the wheelchair and secured it in the trunk.

On the trip to Dr. Atkins' office, we were more optimistic than we had been on our visits to the neurologist, because we had recently made a change. We had decided that Irene should no longer be treated with the steroid, because it was obvious that it was not good for her. She had had numerous infections, lost her eyesight, gained weight, and become confined to a wheelchair. Our doctors had told us that it was what they had expected, that this was how the disease manifested itself, but we were convinced this was the right decision. So our drive to Manhattan was cheerful.

Since Irene had become blind, she had started putting both hands in front of her face, forming a comfort zone to feel more protected. Now, as we drove through the mid-town tunnel, she was in her comfort zone singing our favorite gospel hymn, "This Little Light of Mine." With good spirits, I drove around Manhattan and found parking only a few blocks away from Dr. Atkins' office. Irene removed her hands from her face and waited for me to get the wheelchair, make my way to the passenger door, and repeat my routine of grabbing her by her waist and placing her in the wheelchair.

As we approached Dr. Atkin's place, I noticed that he owned his building. I whispered this to Irene, who removed her hands from her face to hear me. We entered the lobby where there was a huge collection of alternative medicine products. I asked around to find his office, which was upstairs. As we headed to the elevator, Irene was upbeat and enthusiastic.

In the waiting room, we met with nurses, nutritionists, and other health-care professionals, until finally we were called into Dr. Atkins' office. He was taller than I, had gray hair, and was sporting a tan. He was a well-preserved older gentleman. He maintained a calm, professional demeanor as he asked why Irene, who was so young and healthy looking, was in such bad physical condition. Then he asked, "What can I do for you?" after which Irene told him.

While we were in the office with Dr. Atkins, periodically, his staff would come in to let him know there were others waiting. That didn't seem to phase him. He was obviously concerned for Irene, as he told us there was a strong possibility there was a connection between Irene's dental procedure and her condition. He believed Irene's problem could have been due to the overwhelming amount of dental fillings she had. He said that many people felt such fillings contained a poisonous material called amalgam, which could leak into the bloodstream and cause damage. I did not agree. Why weren't all of the others who had fillings affected? But Irene and the doctor discussed the possibility.

At the end of the first visit, Dr. Atkins gave Irene a diet plan, and as we continued to visit, he told us that one reason that he had changed his medical focus was because conventional medicine seemed to be more about treating the symptom than preventing the disease.

On our next visit with Dr. Britton, we told her about the possibility of Irene's dental work being the cause of her neurological damage. She listened and maintained her stance that it was a coincidence, but she did not stop us from trying to find alternative treatments.

After Irene started Dr. Atkins' regimen, she regained the luster in her skin and lost the weight, but she was still in the wheelchair. I had begun to read out loud to her about alternative medicine, and many of the doctors who practiced it were like Dr. Atkins. They had all previously been medical doctors, but had changed their methods because they wanted to help prevent chronic illnesses for which conventional medicine had no cure.

We also read about amalgam—how it was made and what it was made from—and the readings began to open our minds. Learning about the level of mercury and other heavy metals that made up amalgam, raised a red flag for Irene, because since she was a child, the dentist had repeatedly covered her molars with dental fillings. We also learned that our bodies are different, and they react to stress and chemicals differently. Therefore, Irene's body could have been reacting to the toxic amalgam, even though other people had not been affected by it this way.

If that was true, we learned that the process worked something like this: After many years, the toxic substance from the fillings began dripping into her bloodstream, and her body had to adapt to the metal's toxicity. Her need to adapt caused certain neurological cells to allow this metal in the cytoplasm that ultimately changed their ability to function properly, resulting in neurological malfunction of these cells. Further, when Irene had the dental procedure and the root canal, more of the heavy metals and mercury entered her bloodstream, and her body could just no longer take the heavy dose of toxicity.

After all we learned, we could not wait for our next appointment with Dr. Atkins. We had so many questions. When the day came, we arrived at his Midtown Manhattan office on time but waited for him longer than usual. Once we got in, however, I thought that his staff had gotten the idea to clear out the waiting room, because the doctor spent so much time with us. Dr. Atkins, it seemed, regardless of whether his office was full, always gave us his time.

Irene sat next to me with both hands covering her face. The doctor looked at the chart and congratulated her for losing the required weight. But when he asked how she felt, I interjected, and he looked at me as if he could read my mind. Irene then jumped in and told him what we had read about the amalgam, and Dr. Atkins' face broke out in a smile, as if he was pleased that we brought up the subject. Then for the next ten minutes, he spoke to us on the topic, confirming nearly everything that we had read.

After that, he mentioned a group of dentists who removed the amalgam. Dr. Huggins of Colorado Springs, he said, had a treatment for the toxicity of the silver filling. Then he gave us all of the clinic's information and told us to get back to him.

Chapter 25

I, along with Irene and Esther, Irene's younger sister, boarded a plane to Atlanta, where we boarded a smaller plane to Colorado Springs. We landed on Sunday afternoon, rented a car, and stayed at a hotel near the Huggins Center. Our appointment was for Monday morning.

The center was located in a brand new small strip mall among other offices that were still under construction. Across from it were the high mountains. It was late spring, and every half hour or so, it would thunder and rain heavily, and then resume with a bright, sunny sky.

Monday morning, we met the staff at the Huggins Center. The waiting room was full with other patients who were being treated with similar problems. I noticed that most of the patients had traveled from different states and were with their families.

Finally, a modest-looking Dr. Huggins walked into the lobby. He was about my height and looked to be in his early fifties. He spoke to all of the patients and their families, making his way around to us. He introduced himself, and we chatted for a few minutes about our trip from New York.

The family next to us said, "New York, huh? We are from California." The attractive young lady among them mentioned that she was there with her father who had been everywhere, and no one had been able to give them a diagnosis. She said her father was always fatigued, so they'd driven here all the way from California to have her father's amalgam removed.

She also told us that it had been rumored that Dr. Huggins had gotten in a lot of trouble with the American Dental

Association—some even said that he got his license revoked—because he believed that inserting heavy metals such as silver, tin, copper, zinc, and mercury into someone's mouth, though it was mixed with accuracy and precision, led to some chronic illnesses.

I waited in the reception areas as the doctors prepared Irene for the first of many procedures that would take place over the next two weeks. The first step was to remove any remaining corrosive silver fillings. After a short while, one of the assistants came out and asked me to put on a gown, slippers, and a head mask. Irene had asked me to come in because the doctors had decided to remove all of her teeth, and as with all major decisions, we would always go through them together. Once the doctors got in, they realized the extent of the visual corrosiveness of the silver fillings, as well as the deterioration of her remaining teeth It was proof to me that the amalgam had decayed and that the resulting toxicity had caused my wife's condition.

Of all the treatments, the stage I hated the most was detoxification. The doctors gave Irene medication to drink, which would eliminate any trace of heavy metal in her small and large intestines. When Irene had gone to the bathroom enough to clean her of everything, including essential bacteria and vitamins, it was time to replenish, which she did by eating and taking vitamins that the clinic provided.

After all of the treatments were finished, I was concerned and asked a lot of questions. In particular, I wondered, *Did we get here too late?* Though organs can rejuvenate, I was not certain if the nervous system had the ability to restore itself to allow proper communication from Irene's brain to the rest of her body, such as her eyes and her legs. Was it too late for Irene?

I asked her how she felt. "A little weak," she replied. The clinic concluded the treatment with a video of Irene, Esther, and me, as Irene told the story of what she had been through. As I sat there listening to her, I wondered what would be next.

We flew back home to resume our daily routine. Irene's attitude had changed, because she was expecting the treatment to be like a magic bullet that would restore her strength and her ability to see. She looked much better, too, and she was able to stand up from the wheelchair, but she was still not cured.

Finally, figuring that if the treatment was to change her life, it would have done so by now, she had to accept that it was unlikely that she would ever regain her strength. She was dejected. I, too, was disappointed, but also realized that if we had not done the treatment at all, we would have lost Irene. In her situation, there was no doubt in my mind that the damage had occurred from amalgam toxicity.

On our next visit to Dr. Britton, she noted that Irene had made progress. After her routine neurological examination, she concluded that our trip to Colorado had been worth it.

Chapter 26

For four years after she became permanently disabled, we had only Medicare and my job's 1199 union medical benefits. Medicare allowed only health aide services for only three hours a day, although Irene needed much more. Fortunately, the 1199 provided help with the many hospitalizations and medications that Irene needed.

Then, due to Irene's persistence, even after having been rejected several times due to our home ownership and our income, she finally found a way to apply for Medicaid. This enabled her to have a health aide twenty-four hours a day, seven days a week, which we desperately needed.

I did construction on the house to accommodate Irene's condition. I made the doors wider, the kitchen appliances lower, the bathroom handicap-accessible, and a ramp that led from the side door into the backyard.

By this time, all three of our children had graduated from Ronald McNair Elementary and were either in or headed to the private junior high. Despite hard financial times, I would not deny them their education. I had always told them that education was life, that without an education, they would not enjoy life and be able to live it fully.

Those private school days were rough as I paid tuitions, the mortgage, and all the other bills. I found myself on many a Friday afternoon running from the nearby check-cashing place to the school office, just to spare the kids the embarrassment of being pulled out of classes for lack of tuition.

Weekends, we would pack up some food and head to our time-share in the Poconos to enjoy apple-picking, horseback riding, and clean air. We also made several trips to Florida and enjoyed the entertainment parks in the Orlando area.

I worked extra hard to give my children all that they would have enjoyed had their mother not been disabled. And after double and triple shifts, I needed to sleep. After a while, I had to stop sleeping in our bed because the aide had to come in at night to help Irene either turn or take her pain medications.

I moved to a small room next to our master bedroom and put a mattress on the floor, and that was where I slept for many years. I did not like it, but I needed my sleep to be there for the kids and Irene. I would always keep my door ajar so I could hear Irene breathe, and I would rush to the bedroom anytime I noticed she needed help.

In that capacity, my skills as a medical technologist were helpful, and Irene became my patient. I noticed quickly how she felt and oftentimes predicted an infection or an exacerbation, after which I would follow her very carefully and provide her with help before the situation got worse.

I did my best to give my wife care, hope, and encouragement, but it was not easy. Often, I would just sit in the car in our driveway, taking deep breaths, because I knew that my job giving care to Irene and the kids had just begun. Though we had access to twenty-four-seven health care, a few of the aides who were Irene's friends moved on to different jobs after Irene had vouched for them. Others, Irene fired within hours because of a difference in personalities.

We were affiliated with this agency whose job was to assign aides to our home. The aides held twelve-hour shifts, either from 8 AM to 8 PM or from 8 PM to 8 AM seven days a week. Although they helped Irene tremendously, some even going beyond Irene to help the kids with chores, I sometimes felt that I had no privacy because there was always someone there, usually sitting either in the living room or in the dining area when they weren't in the bedroom with their patient.

Sometimes we were lucky to have a health aide who would help us with dinner. But when we didn't, I was the best cook because Irene would come into the kitchen in her wheelchair and coach me. Or, when she was too sick to get out of bed, I would go back and forth between the kitchen and the bedroom to get tips on how to make a well-prepared, delicious dinner for the kids. When dinner was ready, I would serve the kids in the dining room and then take her food into the bedroom, where her bed sat inclined, positioning her plate of food on the hospital-like side table. I or one of the aides would be there while she ate. Sometimes I would sit at the edge of the bed, holding my plate in one hand and spooning away with the other, while we ate together and made conversation.

I was having a hard time taking care of myself, however, because Irene had always taken care of me. She had always made sure I had the proper diet and clean clothes, and now I walked into the room and saw her in desperate need of anyone who could just make her comfortable. To help her, to make her comfortable, required a lot of time, but I did not hold anything back when it came to helping her smile as she sat in her inclined bed, tucking her pillows in around her body so she would not slide down and hit her head against the frame.

It had been many years now since we had gone to the Huggins Center in Colorado. For all those years I had been dreaming that by some miracle her body would stop deteriorating, but her health was never fully restored.

That's not to say she didn't have her better days. She was still able to attend church regularly, where she would sit in her wheelchair, singing and clapping her hands. On other good days, I would take her shopping. Lifting her into our car had been getting more difficult, so I had purchased a customized van with a wheelchair lift installed on the side door. Though she was blind, she would give me details of where the stores were that she wanted to go to, describing them as if she had been there recently, and I would be able to drive there without any problems. Since she had lost her vision, her other senses had seemed to increase, and she would amaze me with how much she picked up on.

This never became so evident, however, as on the day I walked into the bedroom and Irene said, "So tell me. It has been a long time since I have been able to give you some … so, what are you going to do? Tell me, do you have another woman? Because if you do, I will divorce you."

Her tone of voice was insecure, as if she genuinely did not know what my answer would be. I pretended I did not understand the question, because I did not want to respond. I did not want to tell her my secret for all of these years. But then I did, if only part of it. I got close enough to her that we could hear the beats of each other's hearts and told her that I had been closing my door and masturbating.

Due to my stressful life and how I had dedicated my time to working and taking care of Irene and trying to maintain a normal life for the kids, I did not have time for another woman. And even if it had been possible to be involved, I chose to stay with my family and take care of them.

Nothing mattered to me more than my children. I would spend time with them, helping them with their homework. I sent them to various academic centers that would help them with fundamentals in English and math, and I helped them with their science projects, taking them to the school lab to do experiments. I talked to them about drugs, sex, and alcohol, and how people introduced those substances to the young and the curious. I told them that if anyone tried to offer those substances to them, they should run like their lives depended on it. Though Irene was not a physical force in all of this, she was there, and we echoed to them that we were on the same page.

Any spare time I had, I spent at the golf range. Some days I would hit 200 to 400 golf balls. Spare time was easier to find in the warmer months, since, through the camp program offered by my union, my kids were able to go to Camp Thoreau in Vermont every summer.

During one of these kid-free weeks, on a Friday night, I gave in to one of my LIJ coworkers, who had been asking me for months to hang out with him and a few of the guys after work. After all, these were guys I trusted, and they had convinced me that after all of my years walking around LIJ, being so serious, it was time for me to play. Also, because I had been working there since 1980, most people at LIJ knew about Irene's situation and paid me a lot of respect for what I was doing to take care of her and the kids. On the other hand, those who were closer to me had noticed the toll it was taking on me; taking me out for a good time was their way of getting me out of the funk I was in.

We took the Northern Parkway heading east for a while, and then pulled into the front of this inconspicuous place. As we walked up to the entrance, I saw that it was guarded by a gentleman, who said, "Enjoy. And save some money for a tip before you leave."

"What's that about?" I asked one of the guys.

My friend replied, "Oh, that's nothing, man. He is just the look-out for the police."

"Police?" I said. "What ... what the hell is going on, man? Uh–uh, bro, I'm not going in there. I've never been arrested and now is not going to be the first time."

They just ignored me and kept walking toward the entrance. A fine-looking young lady opened the door and welcomed us. She patted me down for weapons, and then she patted my crotch and touched my manhood, saying, "Yeah, baby! You got the weapon we need."

We entered a huge room, much bigger than I had expected, and there was music, a bar area, and some chairs, only a few of which were empty. Though I had never been to a party like this, I was relieved that at least it was clean and orderly. A bunch of guys were looking in one direction where three well-endowed, half-naked ladies were dancing and making provocative, highly flexible moves.

As I took a seat, I noticed a waitress who reminded me of the old days at the playboy club in Dallas, but without the three ladies on poles in the background, one of whom, by then, had gone butt naked. As everyone's attention was on the stage, waiting for the other two girls to follow, I told the waitress, "Heineken."

"Yeah, baby," she replied and moved to her next order.

And then, I don't remember for certain, but surely the next two young ladies dropped everything and continued their routine.

I had never been in a place like this. I hadn't even been with a woman in years. So I was taken by the curvatures, the breast sizes, the lips, thighs, and buttocks. When my friends noticed me finally watching, they gave each other high fives.

Then here came this girl on the stage. With the stage to herself, she began to take off her exotic top. She deliberately made us wait, as one boob came out at a time, her size Ds slowly emerging from underneath. When she had her top completely off, she flexed her huge, perfect boobs, and then continued to take off her mini skirt to sport her perfect, naked body. She turned from front to back and completed her turn. She looked good from head to toe.

As were the thirty or so other guys in the club, I was mesmerized, but instead of getting a hard-on, like I used to in my youth when I would hump on the banana tree, I had the opposite effect. I experienced shrinkage because I was shocked. My penis wanted to hide from what my mind was feeling. It was inexplicable that, after having not been with a woman in so many years, and then looking at this perfect, young, beautiful body, something was holding me back.

Ten minutes later, after she had ended her performance, the girl came up to me and told me she wanted to give me a lap dance.

"Yo, baby," I said, "I can't afford it."

"Don't worry," she replied. "Your friends got you."

I looked at my friends. This was the closest I had been to a woman in a long time, and they were about to enjoy it. I felt more shrinkage. I watched as she pulled one sexy leg and a body measuring 34-28-40, with Ds, over my lap. She squatted and I noticed that her huge, perfect boobs inside her black-and-white polka-dotted halter top. Then I looked down at her matching low-rise bottoms and high-heel boots.

Noticing that I was not comfortable with the situation, she then moved her body to entice me. Honestly, she accomplished her mission. I did not know how to enjoy her and not feel guilty about it, but with everyone watching, I manned up. I closed my eyes to concentrate, but remembering her perfect boobs, the nearly zero-percent body fat on her stomach, and her well-packaged buttocks, I opened my eyes again; I did not want to miss that. That's when she pulled open the latch to her top and her breasts were in my face.

She gave me an added bonus by letting me touch her, but then told me I was squeezing her too hard. I apologized and revealed to her that I had not touched anyone like that for a long time. Then I warmed up and fully enjoyed the next three songs the guys had paid for.

Most nights, I got home within ten to fifteen minutes of the end of my shift. That night, Irene waited for me until 2 AM just to so that she could go to the bathroom. As I picked her up out of the bed, she asked me where I had been. I told her the guys took me out.

"Is that why you smell like cigarette smoke?" she asked.

"Yeah," I replied. "The guys smoked, and I had a Heineken."

I took her from the bed to the handicap toilet bowl and placed her hand at the right spot to insert the catheter and empty her bladder. It took us a while, but she was finally able to sit on the toilet to clean herself and do the self-catheterization. However, I would have to do the rest. As the MS progressed, she had recently become unable to empty out her bowels, so I had to manually remove the fecal content.

Those were my duties that night after I came home from the club. I asked myself, *Why? Why? Why her? She is a good woman.*

In the weeks following the incident at the club, I became increasingly concerned with the future of my two girls. I had now seen firsthand how girls used their bodies for money, and after talking to a few of them in the club that night, I realized that these girls were not on drugs. In fact, the young gem who had given me that lap dance had told me she was in graduate school, and only working there because the moncy paid her tuition.

No way would I allow my two girls to sell their bodies. Now knowing that was an option for many others their age made me talk to my girls. Even though they might need loans to complete their education, I told them, that was a better option to me.

Regardless, I kept the memory of that young gem, whom I would never see again; it was stored for those times when I was lonely and needed to escape my reality.

Chapter 27

It was a bright, sunny afternoon, and Hernst and I were on our way to Sloan-Kettering Hospital in Manhattan. We had gotten word from our younger sister, Martina, that we should come and see our mother, whom she had been caring for since we had lost our father.

We reached the floor where Mom had been admitted due to the recurrence of her cancer. As we sat in her private room, a medical attendant walked in and requested that we talk privately. So Hernst and I followed the resident oncologist to a conference room, where, with no hesitation, the doctor said, "Mrs. Bellevue has a few months to live because she has lost the fight she has been battling. The cancer has spread to her bowels."

He continued to tell us that social workers had already arranged for her admittance into hospice care, and that as soon as a bed became available, Mrs. Bellevue would be transferred. Tears flowed.

After Hernst and I regained our composure, we went back to Mom's room, where uncontrollable tears reemerged.

Mom looked up at us. "Things must be really bad, because two grown men are crying."

I had never showed emotion to my mother, because we were raised to be strong like my father had been. But the pain was too great, too intense for us to bear. It was stressful and difficult to accept the news that Mom was about to die.

A week later, I drove to Calvary Hospital Hospice in the Bronx. It was a clean place with an exceptional staff. I didn't know how they could deal with the fact that most of their patients would die. Mom was surprised to see me wheel in Irene. They hugged and said good-bye. Mom spent three months at Calvary before her death.

A few months had after the funeral, I was lying on my twin-size mattress on the floor in the guest room, thinking about her as I recuperated from a hard day's work. By then, the house had become very busy with nurses and physical and occupational therapists who would make frequent visits to provide care for Irene, and while they were there, I would hide in my room.

One of these times, the health-care aide woke me up. She wanted to show me a small dot that she had noticed on Irene's lower spine. Before even seeing it, I knew exactly what it was. Though we moved Irene on a regular basis, her body had started to develop bed sores.

I looked at it and described how it looked to Irene, and she made an appointment to see a specialist who dealt with wound care. After numerous visits to this specialist, he began to clean out the dead skin, because he said that was the only way the wound would heal. A certified plastic surgeon, he also recommended that he operate on Irene. He explained that Irene had a pressure ulcer, which is when tissue forms over a bony area of her back. Being unable to turn on the bed by herself for so long caused damage to this tissue, and this damage then spread down into the bone. Surgery, the plastic surgeon explained, would allow him to remove the dead tissue and then place healthy tissue, removed from her thigh and buttock, inside the area

We were not sure whether we wanted the surgery right away, so the doctor instructed us to keep the area clean until we decided, using gauze-and-saline packs. For months, we did this, but the wound was not healing. In fact, it was getting larger. It had already gone down into the her spine, and now was spreading lengthwise. It was getting so large that the aides and I had to treat the area twice a day with three or four packs of four-by-four gauze soaked with saline. As she lay on the bed, sometimes urine and feces would get also inside the wound.

It pained me to watch Irene suffer twice a day as we pulled out the pus-covered gauze and replaced it with new packs, so we considered surgery. The risk of her being under anesthesia while having low blood pressure was a concern. But, though the surgery was originally cosmetic to cover her bed sores, it was also now necessary because she was experiencing pain from the open wound. So, we decided to go through with it.

◆ ◆ ◆

Surgery was a success, and after a few weeks, she was discharged. Irene rode home from the hospital in an ambulance, and I followed them in our van. At the house, they carried her on a stretcher and got her gently into her own bed.

A few hours later, I heard our health aide screaming. I immediately jumped up and ran to the bedroom. In an attempt to change the dressing, the aide had turned Irene on her side before removing the old pack. The wound was fully open, and all of the muscle fell out.

I calmed down the aide and explained to Irene what had happened. Irene could only listen, helpless, and I felt we had been taken advantage off. I took pictures that later Hernst advised me to throw out. I called the surgeon, and he had an ambulance come to take Irene to his second location where had been working that day. When she got there, he looked at the wound, removed all of the muscle, and threw it in the garbage. Then he packed the area with gauze and saline solution, and once again, gave us instructions to dress the area three times a day.

The next day, the health aide called and told us that she could not take the pressure and would not be back. Irene talked to her and thanked her for the four years she had been with us, and the agency sent another aide who was so new she had to be trained to work with us.

Later, our regular registered nurse told me that I should sue the surgeon. I didn't pursue it, however, because my main priority was helping Irene to get better. To do that, we went to a wound center located in St. Joseph's Hospital, where Irene had another operation. The doctor successfully closed the area and constructed the flap that the previous surgeon had failed to.

This time, a post-operative bed was not available, but it was worth it, because this doctor was less focused on making money than on the craft of medicine and giving Irene's wound care—unlike the first guy, who was so busy running two private practices that he ignored the little things that meant a lot to patients.

So we ordered a special heated bed made of sand, which Irene lay on when I was to clean her. This flap showed signs that it would survive. So we continued to move her in the bed every two hours until finally it closed, and months later, Irene was able to sit in her wheelchair again.

At one point after that, we had a really good discussion with each other. We mused about the possible causes of MS, as Irene said she had always wondered why she did not have lesions in her brain. We concluded that the toxins had only altered the myelin sheath that surrounded the brain nerves, which sent electrical messages. Because of that, the terrible toxin kept invading her body. So while going to the Huggins Center had reduced the proliferation, it could not stop it.

We also enjoyed the backyard a few more times that summer, having barbecues with close friends. Irene would come out and stay in her comfort zone, taking her hands away from her face every now and then to laugh or reply.

Then, just a few weeks later, while I was away playing golf, Irene exacerbated again. I immediately rushed to the hospital in time to see, from the hallway outside my wife's room, a young doctor inserting a needle into her jugular. He stood behind her as he aimed at a spot on her neck, and then, as he went to insert it, though she was blind, Irene's eyeballs looked as though they were coming out of their sockets.

The MS had attacked her kidneys, and she had become severely dehydrated. Thus, the doctor had to insert a big needle next to a major line so that Irene could get her medication.

Though I knew it was to save her life, it was hard to watch, as he moved it around for a while until it was positioned where he knew he had a major line. I was relieved once he stopped digging and the nurse secured the needle and delivered the medication. I immediately went into the room, and Irene was happy to hear my voice. She was tired and went to sleep.

In addition to everything else, now I would have to manually dialyze her with a tube, which the doctor inserted into her right kidney. As he trained me how to milk it, so I could clean out her kidney, again the flap opened due to a lack of Irene being turned and it being catheterized, and she lay on the opened wound. I complained about the lack of care, only to be told that the reopening of her flap was not a major concern. Irene then asked to be discharged, and we went back to the wound center in Jamaica Queens.

On the Thursday before Mother's Day of 2001, the aide called me as I was getting ready to go to work and told me that Irene had been vomiting because one of the doctors had removed the line from her kidney. I called into work and went to her room in the ICU. Irene told me the doctor had removed the line from her kidney because he thought she did not need it. The doctor had told her that her kidney problems were being caused by her pain medication, so if she stopped the pain medication, she would not have the problem. I wanted to go after the guy, but as Irene lay in the bed of sand that protected her back, she tugged at my hand and told me she was tired. She told me, "It's okay."

Just a week later, after Irene had been discharged from the hospital, the home aide told me that Irene had instructed her not to tell me about her condition. I didn't know what that meant, specifically, so I drew her blood and took it with me to work to test. Again, she was dehydrated. I left work with the permission of my director, met with the ambulance staff, and asked them to take her to the St. Joseph's Hospital wound center.

Irene was so dehydrated that the surgical resident at St. Joseph's could not insert the line in her neck, and the head doctor of emergency medicine cursed the surgical doctor out. That night, Irene was taken to ICU where all of the nurses and doctors recognized her from the previous admission.

I went home, but by the next day, got word that Irene's condition had deteriorated so badly, I asked Salaam to fly in. Then together, Salaam, Latrice, Cherisse, A. J., and I decided that if Irene's heart stopped, we did not want to resuscitate. After all of the pain Irene had been through, we could not prolong her suffering by putting her on a respirator.

Salaam took charge and signed the proxy. I was too weak to sign it because for more than thirteen years I had been totally beaten up.

We spent Mother's Day in the ICU with Irene. It was a beautiful spring day. The May flowers were in full bloom. Normally on a day like today, we would have all been in the backyard after church, putting some marinated ground beef or baby back ribs on the grill. Instead, the family gathered around Irene, praying that she would come out of her coma.

She had been in similar comas and had come out, and we were expecting that she would survive this one. The kids started to softly sing to her, and Irene's eyes opened wide. She then moved her lips like she had many times before when she had wanted me to kiss her. I asked if she wanted something to eat. She shook her head. I asked if she wanted a kiss. She nodded. Latrice, Cherisse, and A. J. watched me kiss her, and then watched her fall back into a comatose state.

A few minutes later, she seemed conscious again. I asked her if I could crush some ice for her. She shook her head. I asked if she wanted some Italian ice, and she nodded. The kids left the hospital, went to the corner store, and came back with the flavored Italian ice.

Then she entertained us and showed us her sense of humor by sticking her tongue out halfway. It was the only body function she had left; the MS had completely paralyzed her.

That evening, as we left the ICU, the kids were happy to have seen a little glimmer of hope.

Then early Monday morning, on Salaam's birthday, my phone rang like it had rung for my dad and mom. But now I was about to bury my wife.

Chapter 28

Six years after I lost the mother of my children, in July 2007, A. J. graduated from DeVry University in Florida with a bachelor of science degree in information technology. The entire family was flying in to attend the ceremony.

I needed a little vacation so I flew to Miami a week early to hang out with A. J. and talk to him about his future. For me and Tara, who I had recently married, I booked a studio villa on the beach, and for the girls, a one-bedroom villa nearby.

A. J. had moved to Florida after graduating from Martin Van Buren High School. We had discussed the program at DeVry with an advisor. I'd felt it was a good program for Arnaud Jr. because, although he could be an A student, he did not typically apply himself to accomplish such goals. The news that he wanted to go to college and get a degree was music to my ears. A. J. had kept his promise, and now three years later it was time for me to congratulate him. I boarded Delta Airlines flight 1862 to Fort Lauderdale and rented a car to meet A. J. at Salaam's residence at Kendall, Miami.

When we greeted each other, A. J. seemed preoccupied. I asked him for directions to Miami Beach from Kendall so that I could check in at Crystal Beach where I would be staying and refresh. A. J. joined me a little later for dinner at an Italian restaurant, where we dined outdoors by a lake and talked about his future. We talked about his plans, how he'd had an offer to work at the place where he'd interned—General Electric—and why he'd refused that position to go work for his brother. As I listened to him plead his case, little did he know that I was elated about his decision.

Salaam and I had already discussed A. J.'s joining his company. He had hoped that A. J. would become successful working with his organization. He'd even given A. J. a salary while he'd attended DeVry. He was scoping him out to see whether A. J. was serious enough about succeeding in his competitive business.

Acting surprised, I became teary-eyed because I was so happy and so proud of him. To change the subject because I felt somewhat awkward with the situation, I picked up a piece of bread from the table and tossed it onto the lake.

"Watch," I said. Sure enough, two midsize red snappers emerged from the water, took bites out of the bread, and swam back down to where we could not see them. A. J. then joined in, and the same thing happened. Then the waiter directed our attention toward a speed boat on the other side of the lake. We observed how the boat was going through the water and making waves. Minutes later, our dinner arrived and we had a wonderful meal and more pleasant conversation.

After dinner, he dropped me off at the villa and headed to his new apartment. It had been an amazing time with A. J.

The next day, I wanted to play golf. I had become interested in golf nearly twenty years earlier when Irene was diagnosed with multiple sclerosis. Our time-share had had a twenty-seven-hole golf course, which I spent time on after popping my Achilles tendon while playing soccer. Then, as we traveled to other country clubs with the kids, I became more interested in golf. In particular, we took several trips to Disney World, and while in Kissimmee, near Orlando, I became devoted to the game. After that, I began to carry my golf clubs on every vacation and always tried to squeeze in a round or two.

The hotel concierge gave me directions to a couple of golf courses. The first one I went to was under construction. So I tried going to the second course and got lost. I missed my turn and ended up a mile farther down the road than I should have.

Meanwhile, I passed the local immigration office, where there was a line of people presumably just entering the country, and ended up in an impoverished community that reminded me of so many others. The disparity of wealth that I saw among the races and ethnicities was also all too familiar: the affluent communities consisted mostly of people of European descent, while nonaffluent communities often contained people of African origin. Life in the affluent area looked vibrant, clean, exciting, and clear; life in the other, crowded, murky, and gloomy.

I circled around before I was able to find the entrance to the second club house, where I was greeted by a young gentleman.

I replied the way I had the many other times I'd been in this situation: "I am a single player, and I would like to play a round of golf."

The gentleman seemed very well trained. He proceeded to tell me what I needed to know to play there without giving me any lines like, "Man, why do you want to play here? Why don't you go back across the bridge where you belong?" Then he told me the price and warned that the golf course was extremely difficult. I presented him with my Platinum American Express credit card for a golf hat and balls that donned the Miami Beach Golf Club logo. I bought them because I was on vacation and because this gentleman had looked upon me with dignity.

I felt welcomed at this golf course and was even allowed to play by myself. I liked playing alone because I teed off several times. I dropped several balls in the rough, and after they landed at wedge distance from the flag, I dropped three or four and practiced hitting the flag. The ground crew looked on and sometimes moved out of my way until I was satisfied with my shots.

When I got to the seventeenth hole after what was an already difficult course for a vacation golfer, the young lady who was driving the vending cart stopped to sell me refreshments. She was a young well-tanned lady wearing fitted shorts, nice sunglasses, and a top that complimented her body. She was very well-mannered. After I collected my change, she said to me, "This is the most difficult hole coming up."

"I have played many challenging holes already," I replied. "You mean this coming hole is more difficult?

"Yeah."

"Why?" I asked.

She looked at the green. "It is above water and protected by bunkers."

I focused on the flag and realized that it would require a precise shot. The architect had designed the seventeenth hole to be difficult for the weekend golfer, elevating the tee box and separating it from the green by a lake. The slightest error would land the ball in the water or the sand bunkers.

I ate my $2.50 banana and sipped the $3.50 bottle of water, as I studied the hole. And when I got to the tee box, I became competitive. I pulled out one of the balls I had purchased, and although the young lady had left, I pictured her there, along with a gallery of others, waiting to see how I was going to play the seventeenth hole, par three, and 175 yards.

I went into my bag and pulled out a six hybrid iron that I had gotten free for accumulating enough points from my American Express card. I knew I had to carry at least 165 yards, so I practiced a swing that I thought would carry the water and the front bunkers.

Then, I approached my shot, and as the ball left my club head, it looked promising. As it sailed over the water, I stood in awe at how perfectly the ball flew toward the flag. Seconds later, the ball landed about fifteen feet from the flag. I had an uphill putt and a great opportunity to birdie that hole. I pulled out my putter, took a few practice swings, and missed the putt to the right, tapping the ball in for par.

I did not have the onlookers I had imagined, but I had one witness: the groundskeeper who had been following me for the past few holes. I noticed his name on his shirt—the same as my brother's—as well as his slight accent. He could have been from anywhere, but I asked him if he was from Haiti. He said yes.

When I told him I was also from Haiti, he paused. I started to speak with him in my Americanized Haitian Creole. He emphasized how much money I had paid to play there. He even included the price of the hat and the refreshment I had purchased. I told him this was a vacation, that I didn't spend that kind of money on a regular basis. Then I double-bogeyed the eighteenth hole and headed to my suite on the beach.

My third and fourth day in Miami Beach, I decided to enjoy the beach. I loved walking the beach. Whether it was in Mexico, the Bahamas, Trinidad, at Myrtle Beach, or in the Dominican Republic, walking the beach always gave me a sense of purging my mind. I watched every wave as it hit the sand and retracted into the ocean, thinking how every single one, although it looked the same as all the others, was very different.

Today, sunbathers were all over, mostly women wearing their swimwear, some of whom took their tops off and were practically nude. Others were just enjoying the beautiful weather. I strolled to my destination, which was nowhere. I looked at my watch; I had been walking for an hour, so I turned around and headed back to where I had started.

The next day, I did the same, only I went in the other direction and walked closer to the waves. I experienced so much pleasure as the waves touched my bare feet; the sensation was delightful. I walked for miles on the sand and near the water. I saw people enjoying the day, sunbathing, swimming, or just sitting and gazing at the sea. A few people were running or walking.

As I strolled, I became amazed at the wealth of the four- to five-star hotels that stretched for miles. I reminisced of Las Vegas and other places I had enjoyed; now for the first time I was able to see them from the back, where patrons enjoyed the beach. Then I remembered the people I had seen waiting in line at the immigration office a few days before, when I had gotten lost on my way to the golf course. They had been people of different nationalities, dressed in the best of what was customary in their respective countries, but all waiting to settle in America. I wondered how different my life might have been had my parents been in that line today.

But because they came during the previous generation, now, I, their son, was able to lie on the sand and walk the beach, just as the new immigrants, with hard work and dedication, would someday be able to give their children a vacation like this.

My dad had been mentally prepared. He'd known what he wanted from America, and it was not to take the easy way out. He could have collected welfare and lived an easier life, but if he had, maybe my attitude would have been different. Maybe if he had, I would have wanted handouts and not had the will to fall on my face, get up, and try even harder.

Instead, throughout the sixties, when the government gave welfare to families like ours, my dad and mom worked. My parents said no to welfare, free housing, health-care benefits, and food stamps, because they wanted to show us that we should not be dependent on that kind of government aid while we are healthy. My dad said no because he knew welfare was the kind of benefit that could lead to generations of dependency. My dad's dream for us was to stand on our feet.

Even on his death bed, my dad said that anything people get free usually is what someone else does not want and, therefore, is not good. To achieve, regardless of the level in which we want to be successful, we must pay a price—hard work and extreme dedication—and my pops showed us how by his example.

I was thankful for my parents, who taught me by example how hard work would eventually turn to good reward, because by following their lead, I was able to achieve all this.

As I walked, sweated, and purged my mind, I felt a funny sensation under my right big toe. I looked at it, thinking I had stepped on something, but I saw nothing. So, I continued toward my suite. A little while down the beach, still about an hour from my destination, the toe started to feel more uncomfortable. I took the pain, digging my toes into the soft sand by the sea. Walking slower now, I decided to put my shirt back on because I was out of sunscreen. Then I began limping to avoid putting too much pressure on my right foot; I did not want to have to call my son to pick me up at the beach. Finally, I recognized a huge hotel that was under construction. Now, I was about a half an hour from the suite.

A long-beaked bird landed in front of me, carrying a fish. The bird began tearing up the fish, plucking its beak into the gills. Then she noticed me walking toward her, so she picked up the fish with her beak and carried it farther ahead. After two or three bouts of this, the bird clasped her lunch inside her claws and flew away, likely to a more peaceful area of the beach.

I made it back after four hours. I was especially proud of not having to call my son. While taking a shower, I saw a giant blister under the sore toe. I would not be able to play golf the next day.

◆ ◆ ◆

Friday morning, I received a call from my daughters. They had landed and were at Salaam's house with A. J.

We all met for lunch at the Cheesecake Factory, and while we waited for our food, Cherisse started sobbing. As we all showed our concern, she told us she was missing her mother, and asked me how I was able to cope and go on with my life. I told her not to feel guilty about missing her mother because she would miss her mother like I missed my parents—both for as long as we lived. I also told her, if nature took its course, some day she would miss me, too. After that, we had a pleasant lunch and made arrangements to meet for Arnaud's graduation on Saturday.

That evening, Tara and her son Jordan flew in, along with Angela and Dave, Irene's long-time friends and A. J.'s godparents. I picked up Tara and Jordan at the Fort Lauderdale Airport. Tara and I had wanted to eat dinner together, because we had been in different places on our third wedding anniversary earlier that week; Tara had already made plans to teach summer school so she had been unable to come with me to Florida. When their flight was delayed, however, we had to cancel.

I had sent flowers to her that day anyway, and when I had returned to the hotel from walking the beach that night, a vase with yellow roses was waiting inside my suite, with a message from Tara saying how much she loved me. I had chuckled and imagined the pleasure she would get when she, in turn, received her flowers from me.

This night, after I picked her and Jordan up from the airport, we drove to South Beach to find that the weekend crowd was out in full force. So we went to McDonald's and then retreated to the suite. She cursed me for being away from her for so long, and she cursed me some more when she cleaned my blister. It was her way of saying she loved and missed me. I was so very happy to see her.

The next day, graduation went as scheduled—A. J. was very jovial at the ceremony—and afterward, we all had lunch at his favorite restaurant. That evening, before we all flew back to New York, we hung out at Salaam's. It was Angela and Dave's first time at Salaam's, even though Angela had known him before everyone else there, because she had been Irene's best friend when he'd been born.

We ate mangoes from his mango trees, reminisced about old times, and talked about the future. We talked about the plan to rename the street were St. Luke Baptist Church was located after Reverend Roy Gilmore. Angela confirmed the ceremony was scheduled for August 26, which was wonderful news because one of the speakers at Reverend Gilmore's funeral had said he would draft legislation for the renaming and he had kept his word. We were so happy that someone we knew and loved was receiving such a distinguished honor in our community.

Though it had been many years since Irene's passing in 2001, her spirit surrounded us as all of her children gathered in her first-born son's house. That we were gathered for A. J.'s college graduation was especially significant, as he'd said his motivation to complete his bachelor's degree was his mom.

You see, the afternoon that I had called the ambulance because Irene's blood tests had indicated dehydration, A. J. had returned from his friend's house just in time to see her go. Irene had been on a special stretcher that would allow the emergency crew to take her down the steps instead of the ramp that went around the back of the house. As they were carrying her out, A. J. asked the EMS woman a question. Noticing him there on the steps, Irene told him that if he had not completed his homework, he should get back in the house and do so. Those were the last words he heard from his mother, and they provided his motivation to complete his degree.

Because Irene had been diagnosed shortly after A. J. was born, he only remembered his mother in a wheelchair. He once told me that he'd grown up believing that that was how she was supposed to be and could not visualize her any other way. Now, at twenty-one, he had obtained his degree because of her, and I was enjoying the fruits: my son's transition to becoming a man.

Heading to the airport that night, I asked Tara, "Honey, how are we getting home from the airport in New York?"

"I made arrangements," she replied.

"Could you share them with me?"

"I already did share them, as a matter fact."

I gasped. "You shared what?"

Tara proceeded to tell me that she had arranged for a limo to pick us up when we landed at La Guardia, which was only a fifteen-minute drive from our house.

I asked her how much the limo ride was costing us, and when she told me, I said, "Are you freaking crazy?" I went on and on until I realized that she had already prepaid.

At the airport, we were greeted by a woman who held up a sign with our name. Then we were escorted to a limo and headed home to Cambria Heights. After everything we had done that week, I truly enjoyed the ride home.

Chapter 29

Salaam had left home shortly after he graduated high school and started his music business. After a lot of hard work, he successfully made several hits. As a result of Salaam's musical success, I attended three GRAMMYs; the first one was back when Irene had still been with us, and it was the only GRAMMY hosted in New York City. Salaam had worked with the Fugees and fellow Croix des Bouquets–born Wycliff Jean (whose album, incidentally, sold over 23 million copies and was nominated for Album of the Year).

Salaam got tickets for all of us, and Latrice, Cherisse, A. J., and I got dressed up and headed to Madison Square Garden. A. J. and I wore our tuxedos, and Latrice and Cherisse their long evening gowns. Irene could not attend, but she coached me about where to go to help the girls prepare for the event, cheered us on as we left our home that evening, and waited up for us with joy. She was so happy for her son and she enjoyed having us attend.

When we got there, the children made it even more fun, as they pointed out all of their favorite artists on the stage.

◆ ◆ ◆

Salaam's professional career was a blessing, and something that had been ingrained in him since birth. He came a long way from playing and singing in the church choir and mixing records in his childhood bedroom. Now, as a producer and executive producer, Salaam had worked with countless artists from Sting to Whitney Houston to Ziggy Marley. He also had the great honor of producing songs that were later certified platinum and multiplatinum.

In addition to his discography, Salaam had an impressive filmography. He was the executive music producer for such blockbusters as *Sex and the City* and *Rush Hour 3*. As a GRAMMY-nominated producer, Salaam was in great demand for not only his past performance but also for his uncanny ability to match music and emotion to create sound.

◆ ◆ ◆

I got a phone call from Cherisse, her voice full of excitement. I asked her to wait a second because I was on the other line waiting for an ER nurse to provide her with critical lab results. Cherisse understood the significance of what I was doing, because she had worked in the lab with me while finishing her BS degree in nursing at Molloy College, where her older sister Latrice had also graduated.

As soon as I hung up with the nurse, I picked up the other line. Cherisse told me that Salaam had just called and said he had been nominated for another GRAMMY. I paused to gather my thoughts and to log in the results I had just gotten, so she repeated herself: "Salaam was nominated for the GRAMMY!"

I knew Salaam's work habits, and I knew he worked with a lot of artists. So I was very happy to hear about the nomination, but I was not surprised. In fact, I had just teased him recently about taking us to another GRAMMY because it had been a few years.

I asked Cherisse who the artist was and what album he was being nominated for. She told me that it was Amy Winehouse, and then reminded me of when we'd first heard her. In A. J.'s freshman year of college, A. J. had come home during a break, and pulled out a demo CD. He told Tara and me to listen to this fresh artist that Salaam had in the studio, then he played "You Know I'm No Good" and gave us a brief description of the singer. He predicted that she would be a big star because she was a talented singer. I could not believe that the track had not even come out and we were among the few selected listeners.

Cherisse concluded her call by telling me that though she was excited for her brother, she could not take the necessary time away from her studies to fly out to Los Angeles to attend this GRAMMY.

I got on the phone with Salaam and confirmed the news I had just gotten from my daughter. Salaam said that the song was something that they had done a few years ago, that the album had done well in Europe, and that now it was in the United States, also doing well. He said the album was being nominated for six awards and asked how many tickets I wanted. I told him that Cherisse could not go but that I would check with the others.

Tara, who was trying to get tenure as a teacher, decided that she could not take the time off to fly out with me. Latrice and A. J. were also doing their thing and could not go. So I called him back to let him know I would be flying out solo.

A few weeks later, Salaam confirmed my ticket, and I gave him my flight schedule so that he'd know when to pick me up from the airport. Then I made arrangements to take off that weekend and fly out to the Fiftieth GRAMMY Awards. I got my Calvin Klein tuxedo and my handmade Modelo Horma colored-crocodile-and-lizard shoes by David Eden. Tara and I picked out a white tuxedo shirt, bow tie, and handkerchief, but when I asked her to pack my *eau Fantasque* cologne, which we had picked up the previous summer on our vacation in the French Rivera, she raised her eyebrows at me. I rubbed my lips on her lips, gave her a Brooklyn kiss, and told her, "There is no one in LA who's got anything on you." Finally, I made an appointment with my barber and went to the health spa for a manicure and pedicure.

The night before my flight, Salaam called and told me that he would arrange for me to get a rented car, because he would not be able to drive me around if I wanted to go anywhere. He described where I would stay in Los Angeles and gave me a list of the essential things I would need during my stay. I told him that a car would not be necessary, that I would be flying out just to support him and his hard work.

The next morning, Tara dropped me off at Kennedy Airport, and I made a nonstop flight to Los Angeles. I stayed at Oakwood in a two-bedroom, two-bath suite, with a dining area, living room, and balcony. It was walking distance to West Hollywood. I did not see Salaam for the first few days, but we spoke on the telephone.

On Sunday, I had breakfast with Salaam, Frank (Salaam's right-hand man and sound engineer), and Gary, who had been working with Salaam in the music industry since the beginning. We were to meet in the garage downstairs from the suite where we would drive to the Staples Center together.

I wanted to take pictures. After all, I didn't know if I would ever get the chance to attend another one of these events. However, it was made clear that no cameras would be allowed. So I made a plan with the driver: when we arrived at the red carpet area, I would hand him the camera while he was opening the door for me. Then, as Salaam and I and his guests walked the red carpet, we would stall and look back, and he would sneak in as many pictures of us as he could.

Approximately twenty blocks from the Staples Center, we had to show a permit that had been issued only to cars going to the GRAMMYs. For security reasons, we went through several other similar posts, where our vehicle was thoroughly inspected.

Finally, we got to the red carpet area, and there were four ushers standing outside to open our doors and welcome us. It was then that I realized my plan for the driver to take my pictures would not work.

The well-dressed lady who opened my door had such a pretty, gentle smile. She nicely welcomed me and said, "No cameras, please." I think she noticed that I was disappointed. I tried to stall to think of another plan that would ensure just one picture.

I decided just to take my time exiting the vehicle. First, I stuck my right leg out of the car, showing only my crocodile-

and-lizard shoes. She stared at them, and then looked at me with her green eyes, as I tried to think of a way to get a picture. She must have known what I was thinking, because as she extended her hand to help me from the vehicle, she repeated with a smile, "No cameras, please."

Clearly, we would be taking no pictures. Nonetheless, it was a pleasant experience to be treated like royalty.

Soon after we started walking, there were cameras all over the place and scores of well-dressed women who welcomed us and wanted to know who among us had been nominated for an award. We all pointed to Salaam, who, meanwhile, was being ushered to an area where interviews were being conducted. I went on, as they indicated for us to keep moving so we didn't disturb the taping.

As we made our way into the Staples Center, again we passed through security before arriving in the lobby. There, we waited until Salaam made his way inside as well. As we proceeded to our seats, I was pleasantly surprised to see how close our seats were to the stage, not to mention how perfectly situated. At this black-tie celebration, I sat on the right side of the stage in section FLR7, row 4, seat 5; this was the section that sat directly behind where all of the artists sat.

We were there a bit early, so many of the artists passed us on their way to their seats. I sat the entire night watching them all, from the new to the old. They were all well-known in the entertainment industry, and I was seeing them in person for the first time. After awhile, though, I felt like one of the rich and famous. I stopped turning my head to see who was passing by. If I happened to see them, it was cool; if not, they just passed by.

During the three or four hours I sat there, I could not help but reflect on how I had gotten to go to two GRAMMYs. Music had always inspired my soul. I liked Brook Benton, Nat King Cole, Gladys Knight, and Aretha Franklin, as well as many Haitian musicians that my parents had used to play on their radio such as Gerard Duperville, Nemours Jean Baptiste, and Jazz des Jeune. I reflected on when Quincy Jones passed, and I remembered being with Irene and Salaam in my room at my parents' house while we talked and listened to Quincy, Herby, Smokey, Gladys, and many other artists.

Music had always just made me feel better. The words inspired me and the messages moved me. When I felt lost and lonely, I used to spin a record and sometimes play it until the needle head on my turntable had to be changed. In those days, the artists sang about love, happiness, and distress.

Salaam's generation was the a new generation of music, the generation of remix. He was born Salaam Remi Gibbs, and went with the name Salaam Remi because the name given to him at birth was so close to the revolution that was happening in music: Remix.

I was observing Salaam now, who sat a few rows ahead of me. Although he had said he did not care whether they won Album of the Year, I could tell he was on edge. He had acted as if he was not expecting the award, but I could tell he was nervous. I knew how important and prestigious the awards were. I knew he would like to add one of them to his long list of accomplishments.

I then reflected on when Salaam played Little League back in Cambria Heights. His mother and I would take him to practices and games. Though one day, Irene had told me that when she alone took him, he did not want to play. So we decided that I would go to games more often. At the next game, I went and gave him a pep talk that I had received from my soccer coaches. He listened to me as we stood by the fence that separated the baseball field from the street and seemed to gain confidence and focus. Then he jogged off to his team with more enthusiasm and athletic posture than I'd ever seen in him.

He played the center field position that day, caught a couple of fly balls, got on base, and scored. He had a good game. The coach told me afterward that he wanted me to be there more often because, until then, he had not known that Salaam was so capable at playing baseball. But I knew Salaam could do whatever he wanted to, if he put his mind to it.

I remembered Salaam hanging out with me and my friends after Victory games and practices. I remembered on Springfield Boulevard, when we still lived in our apartment, when he got his first bike. For days, I had to run behind him and talk to him, and could only let go when he thought I was still there. I remembered going to St. Cleaver Academy with Irene to pick him up while he was in grade school, and dropping him off for the school bus. Those were the days before his brothers and sisters were born.

Now the count was on. Beyonce, with her nice legs and heartbreaking moves, had just finished performing. As we waited still, I couldn't help think that for every Beyonce, tens of thousands of entertainers don't make it. I'd had big dreams and aspirations about sports, dreams that, if realized, could have led me to fame and fortune. But that dream had not been for me. At the same time, although all of these stars around me made exuberantly more money than I did, just being there gave me a sense of my own accomplishments. I was glad I had gone to school and become who I had become. Irene and I had struggled to raise our children, and it was all worth it.

At the time, I had not realized the struggle because it was part of life. One of the kids later put it into words for me by saying, "Dad made it look like everything was normal for us." Now, looking at normalcy, it had become apparent that I had endured a difficult time.

Now, I enjoyed the GRAMMYs in a totally different way than I had at the one nearly a decade before in New York. Then, I'd had three young children with me, and Irene had been at home, willing but unable to attend. Then, all my efforts were on raising my family the best way I knew how. These reflections made me realize that though many criticized my way of life as I neglected myself and gave all I had to ensure the best for my family, I did not back down.

An article that Union 1199 had written about our family in September 1995 summed up the experience perfectly. It stated, "Tragedy struck seven years ago for Irene Bellevue, a former 1199 licensed practical nurse at Kings Brook Hospital in Brooklyn who became a registered nurse in 1977. The Queens mother of four was struck with multiple sclerosis. Several hospitalizations later, she is blind and confined to a wheelchair. Despite the loving care of her husband, Long Island Jewish medical technologist Arnaud Bellevue, and their children, Mrs. Bellevue requires a home care aide twenty-four hours a day."

That article was written to tell our story, the story of a family who had had many dreams and aspirations, only to have them pushed aside. The story also emphasized the commitment I had made when Irene and I married, which was for better or for worse until death do us part.

If I could, I'd have given my seat to Irene tonight, so she could enjoy the fruits of our labor. This day was about the man her son had become, about the things he had accomplished with humor and grace, and about the kind-hearted man that Irene had taught him to be.

Now Alicia Keys was performing "No One," and it brought everyone to a standing ovation. Her talent was so genuine, fresh, and effortless. Her warm and unrelenting beauty, her wonderful voice, and her maneuvering of the keyboard were exceptional. Her performance was heartfelt. She, like Beyonce, gave me goose bumps. On her way back to her seat, she passed us once more, and Alicia was as beautiful in person as she was in pictures.

◆ ◆ ◆

As I sat glued to my assigned seat at the GRAMMYs, most of the successful artists who had received awards had reflected to the past and stated someone who had been significant in their lives. That someone had motivated them to achieve. It made me think.

Salaam had moved out of our house to pursue his career just when Irene had started getting worse. He could have stayed to help care for his mom, but then he would have never known whether he could have accomplished anything in the music business.

At the time, his mother understood that more than I. She had always said that Salaam would make it big.

Only a few years later, when Irene was blind and bedridden, I had come home from work to see her holding a magazine article upside down. As soon as she saw me, she made me read the entire article slowly, word for word. It was about Salaam, and she was the proudest mom. She showed the nurse, the physical therapist, the aide, and everyone else she came in contact with what the magazine said about her son.

To her, he had never left. She was always on the phone with him. When the phone rang and it was Salaam, I could see the love and admiration in her face as she talked to him. When Salaam did not call her, she knew it was because he was overwhelmed, and she just waited patiently. She wanted us to go on with our lives, and she wanted Salaam to be successful. Irene carried the burden of her disease for her children, and now her family could remember her for the strong woman she was.

Chapter 30

The four hours went by and many awards were presented to artists. The album *Back to Black* did very well. Amy Winehouse, a jazz and soul singer, along with producers Mark Ronson and Salaam Remi won five awards.

The album was also going for Album of the Year. This was a highly competitive event because they were competing against Vince Gill who had already won eighteen awards, more than any other male country music artist. In addition, they were competing against albums by Kayne West and Herbie Hancock, a jazz musician.

Little Richard, Jerry Lee Lewis, and John Fogerty then performed the American oldies, music that Irene and I used to enjoy. Their performance got me off my chair.

During a commercial break, the crowd around me stood up to stretch their legs and mingle, but I stayed put. I felt a guiding spirit, one that I had felt before.

It was evident that Irene's spirit was there with us. There were little things that had happened that night that linked Salaam, Irene, and I.

Irene and I used to go to Natalie Cole's concerts, and I would tease her Ms. Cole was the only woman Irene ever had to worry about, because she was my favorite artist. Tonight, Natalie Cole presented the best single to Amy Winehouse. Though this particular song was produced by someone else, Salaam had worked on the album. And when Amy appeared on the satellite screens and made her speech, she mentioned our son.

As the night wore on, I felt as if Irene's spirit were fading away, and with a pleasant smile, I felt her there with Salaam and me. I couldn't help but embrace her spirit. By the end of the GRAMMYs and as her spirit faded I got the overwhelmed feeling of her telling me in her usual way, "You're deep, brother man. Job well done."

For the first time since she passed away, we connected at this spiritual level, and it gave me a sense that we could all go on with our lives, because I knew she was in a place where she could always enjoy us.

Having that spiritual connection shined the light on me. It made me realize that we all have our destiny, we all are blessed and successful with God-given talent, and we must accept our purpose to do a job well done.

Epilogue

It is a good thing that I live in America; I had a second and a third chance to do life in a way that was productive, both for me and my family. Those who used to sympathize with my struggle always told me, "God will bless you." I do feel blessed to have a family who loves me.

I got yet another chance at life with the opportunity to be remarried, in July 2004, to a wonderful woman who understood me and the struggles I faced.

For my fifty-first birthday, Tara and the kids threw me a surprise birthday gala. It must have taken months, with everyone working endless hours for this party to happen, especially Tara, who made the decorations as well as a pamphlet that provided a synopsis of my life.

All were involved in keeping it a secret, and the night of the party, they made me believe I was going to a wedding. Tara wanted me to wear a tie but would not tell me why.

It turned out wonderfully. Many of my old-time friends were there. Salaam, who could not be there because of his busy schedule, called within minutes of its start to wish me well. In addition, several people wrote letters and poems for me, which I will share with you now in closing.

Tara wrote the following poem:

The Golden Path

Take my hand this way we'll go,
Said God so gently.

I'll take you to a place of joy,
Where you will find true love.
When you feel that you are lost,
All you have to do is pray,
And I'll be there once again,
To help you on your way.
I did pray and just as said,
He shined his light from above,
That showed me the way down the golden path,
That led me to your love.
To Arnaud's love so pure, so true, so real
Hand and hand as we walk down
The golden path of eternity.
Love Always,
Tara Bellevue

Jordan, Tara's son, wrote this:

You are the man that makes my mom happy
You are a husband, father, and friend
You are the head and the whole
You are the man who someone can count on
You are the sun that shines so bright
You are the man who makes sure everyone is happy
You are who you are and let no one come in between that
You are a teacher who guides people on the right path
You are the man who follows his own path
You are the man who works hard
You are the man who never gets any sleep and still makes it to work on time
You are a hero and a leader—strong, caring, and loving
This is who you are and let no one come in between that!!!!!

My brother, Hernst, and Yanick, his wife of thirty-five years wrote:

A Prayer for You

As Benjamin Franklin said, "A brother may not be a friend, but a friend will always be a brother." Yanick and I are blessed to have you as a brother and a friend. As you celebrate your fifty-first birthday, may the grace of God continue to enflame your compassionate heart and lead you to understand that "through wisdom the house is built, and by understanding it is established; by knowledge the rooms are filled with precious and pleasant riches" (Proverbs 24:3-4). As you are enjoying this wonderful moment surrounded by true friends, may God bless you for fifty-one more years!

My first-born daughter wrote:

A Love Letter to Daddy

To the best father I know...
To the hardest working man I know...
To the most dedicated person I know...

Daddy, I love you so much! I know it's not easy to work as hard as you do to support us, but somehow you manage to do so. I admire you so much for that. You have taught me so many things, such as study now and play later, it is important to have a career instead of having a job, the importance of family, and lastly in your words "I've done that before you were born."

It has been a hard journey. But we still have each other. Losing Mommy was the hardest thing I have ever faced. Thank you for never leaving us behind and keeping our family together. You are priceless.

On your fifty-first birthday, I want to wish you as much happiness and joy as your heart can hold. These are your golden years. Enjoy them! Just take us for the ride once and awhile.

I feel so blessed to have the genes of two of the most intelligent, wonderful, caring parents anyone could ask for. With that said,

I will end with this: Daddy, you may not be perfect but you are perfectly chosen!

Thank you for choosing us!
Love, Latrice

My middle daughter, Cherisse, wrote:

He is...

When life throws you a curveball
And there is no place to go but down
I've always watched him stand tall
Floating away from the ground
Keeping his head high
And his spirits even higher
Tackling every obstacle with pride and fire
His intensity never expires
As a child I knew he just had to be Superman
Doing so much and never taking time to take a bow
Instead continuing the race when his shoes were filled with sand
And still able to give us all the luxuries of a child
He gives so much and takes so little
Holds so many hands
Without showing the middle
As he accommodates countless demands
His labor load is long and hard
Yet his hugs are warm
His eyes sparkle like stars
While his smile is never gone
He is one of a few
Deserving of every ounce of praise
He is my dad and my inspiration:
Arnaud Jean Bellevue

My son A. J. wrote:

Ode to Daddy

What makes a man a man?
Must he be 51?
Should he have a mustache?
Should he have a wife?
What makes a father a father?

He should provide for his young.
He should love his family.
He should work to make sure those whom he loves prosper.

But what if he does all of this and then some?
What if he works five double shifts, and still wakes to take his son to play baseball?

What if his wife is sick and he is forced to handle most of the house expenses on his own?

My father is not just a man he is way more than that;
My father is a human being with a heart the size of life.
My father is a warrior put on this earth by God to ensure that my family and I succeed.

The world is lucky to have him as a member.
I am lucky to have him as my father.
I love you, Dad.

Tara read this to me at the birthday party:

The Man (author unknown)

The man who is my friend, my lover,
my protector, and my consoler.
The man who brings me joy.
The man who I will love through eternity.
The man who is admired and respected
The man who is the captain of our ship, S.S. FAMILY
The man, the husband, the father and the friend.

Those were some heartfelt words coming from people who I have truly loved and who mean a lot to me. The night was truly special.